Aztec and Maya
Myths

Acknowledgements

I am grateful to Dr Stephen Houston of Vanderbilt University, Dr Mary Ellen Miller of Yale University and Nina Shandloff, Senior Editor of the British Museum Press, for their perceptive comments and suggestions during the preparation of this book. I am indebted to Justin Kerr for generously providing the cover photograph, and I also want to give special thanks to the Akademische Druck-und Verlagsanstalt, Graz, for granting permission to publish photographs from their fine facsimiles of Mesoamerican codices. Dr Iain Mackay of the British Museum provided much appreciated assistance with the photographic archive of the Museum of Mankind. I wish particularly to thank and credit Dr Emily Umberger of the University of Arizona, Tempe, for providing her line drawing of the Aztec Calendar Stone, and my late grandmother, Alice Wesche, for her drawing of the Maya death god ballplayer figurine.
The direct quotes from particular colonial texts are drawn from the works of Miguel León-Portilla, Arthur J. O. Anderson and Charles E. Dibble, Dennis Tedlock, Alfred M. Tozzer, Ralph L. Roys, and Munro S. Edmonson. At times, their original text has been altered slightly in order to be consistent with the spelling and punctuation used in the present volume. Details of each of these sources are given in the suggestions for further reading.

THE · LEGENDARY · PAST

Aztec and Maya
Myths

KARL TAUBE

Published for The Trustees of

The British Museum by

BRITISH MUSEUM PRESS

Published by British Museum Press
A division of The British Museum Company Ltd
46 Bloomsbury Street, London WC1B 3QQ

First published 1993
Reprinted 1995, 1998

British Library Cataloguing in Publication Data
A catalogue record for this book is available
from the British Library

ISBN 0–7141–1742–0

*The great city of Teotihuacan,
birthplace of the sun and
moon in Postclassic central
Mexican myth.*

Designed by Gill Mouqué and Diane Butler
Cover design by Slatter-Anderson
(Photograph courtesy of Justin Kerr)

Typeset in 10½ pt Sabon by BP Integraphics Ltd, Bath
Printed in Great Britain by The Bath Press, Bath

FRONT COVER *The maize god, flanked by his
sons Hunahpu and Xbalanque, emerging out of
the earth, represented as a split turtle shell.
Detail of a Late Classic Maya bowl.*

Contents

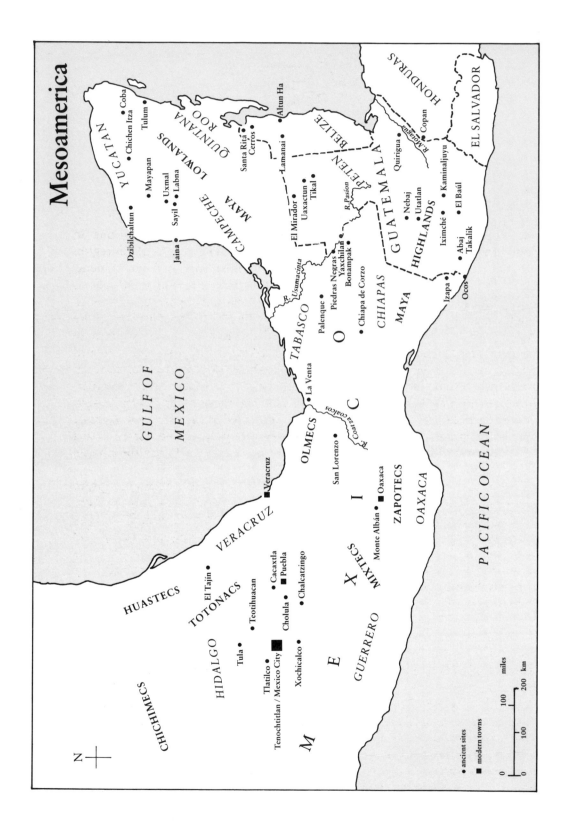

Mesoamerica

GULF OF MEXICO

PACIFIC OCEAN

HONDURAS

EL SALVADOR

YUCATAN

QUINTANA ROO

CAMPECHE

BELIZE

PETEN

GUATEMALA

HIGHLANDS

CHIAPAS

MAYA

MAYA LOWLANDS

TABASCO

OLMECS

VERACRUZ

HUASTECS

TOTONACS

HIDALGO

MIXTECS

GUERRERO

ZAPOTECS

OAXACA

CHICHIMECS

M
E
X
I
C
O

Coba
Chichen Itza
Tulum
Altun Ha
Santa Rita
Cerros
Lamanai
Mayapan
Uxmal
Labna
Sayil
Dzibilchaltun
Jaina
El Mirador
Uaxactun
Tikal
R.Pasion
Copan
R. Motagua
Quirigua
Nebaj
Kaminaljuyu
Utatlan
Iximché
El Baúl
Abaj
Takalik
Izapa
Ocos
Piedras Negras
Yaxchilan
Bonampak
Chiapa de Corzo
R. Usumacinta
Palenque
La Venta
R. Coatzacoalcos
San Lorenzo
Monte Albán
Oaxaca
Veracruz
El Tajín
Cacaxtla
Puebla
Teotihuacan
Cholula
Chalcatzingo
Tula
Tlatilco
Tenochtitlan / Mexico City
Xochicalco

N

- ancient sites
- modern towns

miles
100

km
200

100

100

0
0

Introduction

Although 1492 marked the initial contact between New World peoples and Renaissance Europe, it was not until the early sixteenth century that Spanish explorers first encountered major native civilisations in southern Mexico and neighbouring Central America. The peoples of this region inhabited great cities with complex forms of administration and government, employed intricate systems of writing and calendrics, and celebrated refined poetry, music, dance and art. Unfortunately, it was not sophisticated culture but the promise of gold and riches which drew the first Europeans. In 1521 the Aztec capital of Tenochtitlan was conquered and looted, and only a minute fraction of its treasures were preserved or recorded for posterity. While in Brussels in 1520, the German artist Albrecht Dürer examined Aztec material previously sent by Hernán Cortés to King Charles v: 'All the days of my life I have seen nothing that rejoiced my heart so much as these things, for I have seen among them beautiful works of art, and I marvelled at the subtle intellects of men in foreign places.' Although little understood by Dürer, these same works of art portrayed complex modes of thought no less refined than the objects themselves.

It is easy to lament the massive destruction of screenfold books, sculpture and other native works at the time of the Spanish conquest, but a far more profound cultural loss was the destruction of indigenous customs and beliefs by death and disease, slavery and mass conversion. However, although a great deal of the mythology presented in this book derives from those few precious works now carefully preserved in major museums and libraries around the world, this is by no means a description of dead gods of a vanished people; much of the mythology survives to this day in the beliefs and speech of the living descendants of the Aztecs, Maya and other native peoples of Mexico and Central America.

The region occupied by the ancient Aztec and Maya, now commonly referred to as Mesoamerica, is an area encompassing southern and eastern Mexico, all of Guatemala, Belize and El Salvador, western and southern Honduras, and the Pacific side of Central America as far south as the Nicoya Peninsula of Costa Rica. Ancient Mesoamerican peoples shared a series of cultural traits; among the most striking are two calendars of 260 and 365 days that permutate in a great cycle approximating fifty-two years, hieroglyphic writing, screenfold books and masonry ballcourts with rings. Although the peoples inhabiting this area were of many distinct cultures, often speaking mutually unintelligible languages, none the less there was widespread contact over millennia through migration, trade, conquest and pilgrimage. It is therefore not surprising that many themes are shared between the mythologies of the Aztec, Maya and other peoples of ancient Mesoamerica.

Certain gods, symbols and mythical episodes described in this book may appear strikingly similar to Old World examples, yet they derive from independent development, and no evidence exists of any exchange between Old and New World civilisations prior to the sixteenth century. Along with all other native New World peoples, the inhabitants of Mesoamerica arrived by crossing the Bering Strait between Siberia and Alaska near the end of the Ice Age. Indeed, certain Mesoamerican beliefs, such as shamanic transformation, a lunar rabbit, and the importance of world directions and trees, do suggest a link to eastern Asia and may well have been introduced by these first immigrants, perhaps as early as the tenth millennium BC.

Ancient Mesoamerican history

In comparison with Sumer, Egypt and other early civilisations of the Old World, those of Mesoamerica are of relatively recent origin. The Olmec, the first great culture of the region, and perhaps the first to warrant the term civilisation, developed in the tropical lowlands of southern Veracruz and neighbouring Tabasco. By the twelfth century BC the Olmec were constructing ceremonial architecture and monumental sculpture representing a complex iconography of cosmology, gods and symbols of rulership. Like later Mesoamerican societies the Olmec economy depended on farming, especially maize – still the most important crop in Mesoamerica today. Another early civilisation, that of the Zapotec of highland Oaxaca, inscribed the earliest known instances of calendrics and writing in the region, and by 600 BC they were recording calendrical information of historical significance. The mountain city of Monte Albán served as the Zapotec capital for well over a thousand years. Whereas Olmec culture ended by 400 BC, the Zapotec remain one of the major native groups of contemporary Oaxaca.

The Protoclassic period (100 BC–AD 300) marks the development of complex urban cultures over much of ancient Mesoamerica. In the Maya region of eastern Mesoamerica, the lords of such sites as Izapa, Abaj Takalik, Kaminaljuyu, El Mirador, Uaxactun and Tikal began erecting impressive monumental art and architecture. At Izapa, in particular, many stone monuments clearly portray mythological episodes.

Although known to the Protoclassic Maya, writing achieved an especially high level of complexity and importance during the following Classic period (AD 300–900). As a result of deciphering Maya glyphs, one can today voice the actual Mayan names of gods, cities and kings. In addition, abundant texts and art graphically portray many aspects of Classic Maya mythology. Because of the artistic and architectural achievements at such sites as Palenque, Yaxchilan, Tikal and Copan, the Classic period is commonly regarded as the apex of Maya civilisation. The inhabitants of these and other sites clearly shared similar

Olmec celt figure, ground stone axe head (Museum of Mankind, London), Middle Formative period, c. 600 BC.

beliefs, although there is no evidence that the Classic Maya were ever unified in a single empire or confederation. Instead, the picture appears to be one of competing city states, and by the end of the Classic period many Maya sites had been abandoned. However, this was not the end of Maya civilisation; its greatest known epic, the *Popol Vuh*, came from the pen of a sixteenth-century Quiché Maya. Indeed, sacred narrative continues to be a vigorous tradition among modern Maya peoples, although the main focus of this book is pre-Hispanic Maya mythology.

One site in particular, which rose to prominence during the Protoclassic period in central Mexico, was known by the later Aztec as Teotihuacan, meaning 'place of those who became gods'. This is where the sun and moon were created according to the mythology of the Aztec, who named its two greatest pyramids after the sun and the moon. The largest of these, the Pyramid of the Sun, was constructed about the beginning of the Christian era. This massive structure directly overlies a natural cave – a possible reference to the emergence of people out of the earth, a well-known creation episode in later Mesoamerica. At its height in the Classic period, Teotihuacan covered over 20 square kilometres (some 8 square miles) and contained a population of perhaps 200,000. The city's plastered walls were covered with brilliant mural paintings, many of which depict gods known to the subsequent Toltec and Aztec cultures of central Mexico.

By the beginning of the Early Postclassic period (AD 900–1250), Teotihuacan, Monte Albán and many Maya sites were virtually abandoned. The central Mexican site of Tula, which dates from this period, is now known to be the legendary Tollan, the capital of the Toltecs ruled by Topiltzin Quetzalcoatl – human counterpart of the great god Quetzalcoatl. According to both central Mexican and Yucatec Mayan texts, Quetzalcoatl moved his capital to the red lands of the east, quite probably Yucatan. The site of Chichen Itza, in Yucatan, exhibits strong and specific Toltec traits, and clearly this site shared a very special relationship with Tula during the Early Postclassic period.

The Late Postclassic period (AD 1250–1521) corresponds to the cultures encountered by the Spanish in the sixteenth century, and virtually all of the

The rain god Tlaloc carrying maize. Detail of Teotihuacan mural, Classic period.

Tula, Hidalgo, the legendary Toltec city of Tollan. Early Postclassic period, c. AD 900–1250.

known surviving pre-Hispanic screenfold books date from this time. Moreover, early colonial works composed by both Spanish and native scholars provide a wealth of documentary material on Late Postclassic customs and beliefs. Whereas the Maya are best known for the Classic era, the Aztec epoch is wholly within the Late Postclassic period. The Aztec, or Culhua–Mexica as they preferred to call themselves, were relative newcomers to central Mexico. Their great island capital of Tenochtitlan – future site of Mexico City – was not founded until approximately 1345. None the less, by the time of the Spanish conquest, less than two centuries later, the Aztec had created the greatest empire known in ancient Mesoamerica.

The origins and growth of the Aztec state are strongly reflected in Aztec religion. As a means of legitimisation, the Aztec aggressively adopted the beliefs and iconography of earlier peoples. For instance, the site of Tula, the legendary Toltec capital, was accorded special prominence, and certain Aztec gods can be traced back to Tula and still earlier Teotihuacan. The Aztec also incorporated religious practices from contemporaries, including peoples of Puebla, the Gulf Coast Huastec and the Mixtec of Oaxaca. The conscious adoption of foreign customs both solidified conquest and offered cultural unification; the Aztec even had a special temple, the Coateocalli, which contained the captured images of foreign gods. Although Aztec mythology thus has many deities and themes derived from other Mesoamerican cultures, certain myths are wholly Aztec – particularly the mythic origins of Huitzilopochtli at Mount Coatepec, which served as a sacred charter for the expansion of the Aztec state.

The founding of the Aztec capital of Tenochtitlan. Codex Mendoza, f. 2r, early colonial period. In the centre stands an eagle on a flowering nopal cactus and a rock (the place-name of Tenochtitlan). According to Aztec migration accounts, the eagle and cactus served as a sign and omen for the future capital of the Aztecs.

The day Ce Cipactli, or 1 Caiman. As the first day of the 260-day calendar, 1 Caiman is widely associated with beginnings and creation in Mesoamerican mythology. Detail from stone box, Aztec, Late Postclassic period.

Ancient Mesoamerican religion

Calendrics

In pre-Hispanic Mesoamerica, calendrics played an essential role in mythology as well as in daily life. One of the most important cycles was the calendar of 260 days, composed of twenty consecutive day-names combined with the numerals one to thirteen. For example, a given day such as 1 Caiman was formed of two parts: the numeral 1 with the day-name Caiman. A particular day would not repeat until all 260 combinations of day-names and numerals were played out. In ancient Mesoamerica individuals, gods and even world epochs were often named by this calendrical cycle. Thus the legendary ruler of Tollan, Topiltzin Quetzalcoatl, was also named by the day 1 Reed, or Ce Acatl in the Aztec Nahuatl language. In a similar vein, many of the gods mentioned in the Maya *Popol Vuh* creation epic possess names drawn from the 260-day calendar. Although of less importance in native mythology, Mesoamericans also tracked a vague-year calendar of 365 days composed of eighteen twenty-day months with a final period of five days. The 365-day vague year ran concurrently with the 260-day cycle, with each vague year being named by a specific 260-day date. Due to the permutations of these two cycles, a particular named vague year, such as 2 Reed, would not recur until the completion of fifty-two vague years.

Still another calendrical system was favoured by the Maya and neighbouring peoples of south-eastern Mesoamerica. Known as the Long Count, this vigesimal system (based on the number twenty) consisted of a constant count of days from a mythical event in 3114 BC. Although first known among non-Maya peoples in the first century BC, this system was developed to its highest level of complexity and popularity by the Classic Maya. An abridged form of the Long Count continued in use well into the colonial period among Yucatecan-speaking peoples of the northern Maya lowlands.

In Mesoamerican thought, the calendar concerned the definition and ordering of space as well as time. Each of the twenty day-names of the 260-day calendar was oriented to a particular direction, passing in continuous counter-clockwise succession from east to north, west and finally south. Similarly, the

A Mesoamerican model of time and space. Gods, day-names, trees and birds are oriented to the four directions, with Xiuhtecuhtli in the centre. Codex Fejérváry-Mayer, p. 1, Late Postclassic period.

365-day years also moved in a counter-clockwise succession from year to year. Page one of the Fejérváry-Mayer Codex depicts the 260-day calendar oriented to the four directions with associated birds and trees. The central Mexican god of fire and time, Xiuhtecuhtli, stands in the centre of the scene as a warrior backed by four streams of blood. The source of this blood appears near the four birds at the outer corners of the page: it originates from the severed arm, leg, torso and head of Tezcatlipoca, one of the greatest gods of central Mexico. Although this precise mythic episode is not known from other sources, the scene suggests that the casting of Tezcatlipoca's dismembered body to the four quarters by Xiuhtecuhtli was tantamount to the creation of the calendar and directions – that is, the delineation of time and space.

Mesoamerican calendrical systems were not simply used to delineate thirteen-day weeks, twenty-day months, vague years and other periods of daily reality. They also distinguished intervals that were especially charged with sacred and often dangerous powers. The peoples of ancient Mesoamerica keenly observed the sky and used the calendar to predict solar and lunar eclipses, the cycles of the planet Venus, the apparent movements of constellations and other celestial events. To them, these occurrences were not the mechanical movements of innate celestial bodies but constituted the activities of gods, the actual recapitulation of mythical events from the time of creation. In central Mexico, the first appearance of Venus as the Morning Star was Tlahuizcalpantecuhtli, Lord of the Dawn, who battled the rising sun at the first dawning at Teotihuacan. The calendrical cycles themselves also delineated sacred moments of time. The vast majority of Classic Maya stone monuments celebrated the completion of major Long Count calendrical periods. Among the Postclassic Maya of Yucatan, the end of the 365-day vague year was an especially dangerous time and, according to the colonial *Cantares de Dzitbalché*, was equivalent to the destruction and re-creation of the world. Thus much of the imagery in the Yucatec new year rites also appears in Maya creation mythology. Similarly, the completion of the Aztec fifty-two year cycle was marked by an anxious vigil: if new fire was not successfully drilled, the terrifying star demons of darkness, the *tzitzimime*, would reassert their control over the world.

Day versus night

The contrast of night and day constitutes one of the most basic oppositions of Mesoamerican thought. Native accounts of the first dawn describe this event as the origin of the legendary and historical time of mortals, in contrast to the mythical period of creation. Thus in the Quiché Maya *Popol Vuh*, the gods and fierce beasts become stone at the first appearance of the sun. Similarly, according to one Aztec account, Tlahuizcalpantecuhtli turns into the god of stone and

The Venus god Tlahuizcalpantecuhtli attacking a watery mountain or altepetl, the Aztec term for town. Detail of Venus pages, Codex Cospi, p. 10.

15

cold at the first dawning at Teotihuacan. In Aztec myth, the gods were sacrificed during the dawning at Teotihuacan and, according to one version, sacred bundles were made from their remains. Both the Aztec and Maya accounts explain the origins of the later condition and appearance of the gods, who in reality were represented in inert stone sculpture or wrapped in sacred bundles.

Whereas dawn marks the daylight period of stability and order of daily mortal existence, the night corresponds to the mythic time when gods and demons come alive. According to modern peoples of Veracruz, once the sun sets, only the night stars keep rocks from turning into jaguars. In Mesoamerican belief, the night is when form-changers and other demons prowl. The dark nocturnal hours are also a special time when mortals communicate with the supernatural. During dreams, one's spirit familiar performs hazardous journeys to meet ancestors, gods and other supernatural beings. The night is also the preferred time for consuming psilocybin mushrooms, peyote, morning glory seeds and other hallucinogens in order to communicate with the spirit world. Above, in the night sky, the sacred episodes of creation are continually played out in the apparent movements of constellations and planets. Solar eclipses are especially feared, since they constitute the violent reassertion of the stars and other night beings over the day.

Although there is a contrast between the chaotic nocturnal hours and those of the day, it is by no means a simple distinction between good and evil. In Mesoamerican thought, such dualistic principles tend to be considered in complementary opposition: both are required for existence. Just as sleep is a necessary revitalising counterpart of daytime activity, the night and sacred time infuse daily reality with renewed power and force. The junctures noted in calendrical periods correspond to those times of rejuvenation when the forces of creation recur. This sacred mythic time can penetrate into daily existence through ritual and omens, and even by the presence of actual living individuals such as kings, priests and shamans, curers and twins.

Twins

Twins are commonly regarded with a certain apprehension in Mesoamerica where, much like monster births, they are feared as strange and abnormal portents of religious significance. In central Mexico the canine god Xolotl was god of both twins and deformities. According to the Dominican Fray Bartolomé de las Casas, Aztec twins posed a mortal threat to their parents and for this reason one of the pair would be slain at birth. However, the fear of twins involves more than parental well-being, for they also embody the mythic time of creation. Twins are widely found in the creation mythology of the Aztec, Maya and other Mesoamerican peoples. Quite commonly they serve as monster-slayers and culture heroes who create the environment and materials necessary for human life. But just as they are the creators of order, they are also the embodiment of conflict and change.

The Quiché Maya *Popol Vuh* contains a detailed account of the hero twins Xbalanque and Hunahpu, who descend to the underworld to avenge the deaths of their father and uncle (also twins). In central Mexico, the culture hero Quetzalcoatl is identified with twins, and the concept is even contained in his name since in Nahuatl the term *coatl* signifies both 'twin' and snake. Quetzalcoatl is often paired with Xolotl or Tezcatlipoca in Aztec creation mythology. Although not as explicit as the Quichean Hunahpu and Xbalanque, these pairings also allude to the concept of hero twins. The motif is clearly of great antiquity in the New World; aside from Mesoamerica, hero twins are commonly found in the creation mythology of neighbouring Central America, lowland South America and the American Southwest.

LEFT *The Classic Maya forms of the Popol Vuh hero twins, Hunahpu and Xbalanque. Painting from Naj Tunich Cave, Guatemala.*

Mosaic sacrificial knife. Aztec (Museum of Mankind, London), Late Postclassic period.

Role models and social conduct

Mesoamerican myths are more than sacred accounts of the origins of the world; they also contain profound lessons for proper behaviour. Among the most commonly mentioned vices to bring disaster or defeat are arrogance and greed. In Aztec mythology it is not the vain and wealthy Tecuciztecatl but rather the humble yet brave Nanahuatzin who eventually becomes the sun. In the *Popol Vuh*, the hero twins slay the monster bird Vucub Caquix because of his excessive pride and bragging. Arrogance and avarice are vices common to high office, and a great deal of the preserved mythology provided models for royal conduct. However, Aztec and Maya mythology also address broader and more profound matters, such as the meaning of human existence. According to the *Popol Vuh*, the gods create the present race of humans, the people of maize, to supply sustenance to the gods in the form of prayer and sacrifice. Similarly, the accounts of sacrifice of the gods at Teotihuacan and the killing of Coyolxauhqui and her brothers describe the necessity of human sacrifice for the continuity of the world. Although this continues to be the most vilified aspect of ancient Mesoamerican religion, human sacrifice arose out of a basic premise, a recognition of the active role and responsibility of people for the maintenance of cosmic balance.

Major sources and the history of research

Like other peoples of ancient Mesoamerica, the Aztec and Maya were literate and recorded their mythologies in a wide variety of media, including screenfold books, painted vases, carved wood and bone, and monumental stone carving. But equally important are the accompanying images, which illustrate mythical episodes and the attributes of particular gods.

The pre-Hispanic screenfold books, commonly referred to as codices, have been essential for the study of native religion. Sadly, only some eighteen books in pure native style have survived. Just four Postclassic screenfold books exist for the Maya: the Dresden, Madrid and Paris codices, and a fourth recently discovered book, the Codex Grolier. For central Mexico, there is an especially important series of five manuscripts: the Borgia, Vaticanus B, Cospi, Laud and Fejérváry-Mayer codices. Named after the most impressive of these screenfold books, the Borgia Group is painted in a style typical of Late Postclassic central Mexico. However, the precise provenance of this group is unknown, and it is unlikely that they derive from a single locality. Whereas the Codex Borgia itself may well have come from the state of Puebla, Veracruz has been suggested for the Laud and Fejérváry-Mayer. Although these manuscripts may have originated in regions under Aztec control, body proportions and other conventions indicate that they were probably not painted at the Aztec capital of Tenochtitlan. None the less, the religious meanings and content of the Borgia Group confirm and amplify what is known for the Aztec.

The nine extant Maya and Borgia Group of codices are primarily divinatory manuscripts used with the sacred calendar. The gods usually appear in relation to specific auguries and rarely in sequential narratives. For this reason, these pre-Hispanic codices usually contain only tangential references to mythological episodes, with the one noteworthy exception being the poorly known middle pages of the Codex Borgia, portions of which correspond to recorded Aztec myths. Although these nine codices are divinatory, other pre-Hispanic books concern mythology. An example is the obverse of the Codex Vindobonensis, which describes creation events including the origins and history of 9 Wind, the Mixtec form of Quetzalcoatl. Unfortunately, no such pre-Hispanic manuscript survives for the Aztec or Maya. However, some colonial mythological accounts written in Latin characters seem to have been transcribed from pre-Columbian books. According to the early colonial Quiché writer of the

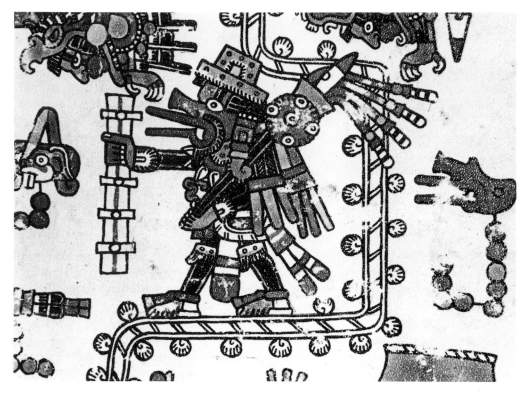

God 9 Wind, the Mixtec form of the wind god Ehecatl-Quetzalcoatl. Codex Vindobonensis, p. 48 (detail), Late Postclassic period.

Popol Vuh, this Maya manuscript derived from a lost ancient book, and certain mythological accounts pertaining to the Aztec were also transcribed from now-lost pre-Hispanic codices.

The most important sources for Aztec mythology derive not from the pre-Hispanic era, but from the early colonial period. Whereas many Spanish colonists considered the native population primarily as a source of brute labour and tribute, the Franciscan, Augustinian and Dominican religious orders saw these peoples as a utopian opportunity to create a new and better world. Rather than denigrating the ancient achievements of the Aztec, they saw these works as proof of an innate ability to achieve greatness. As humans possessing rational souls and the capacity for civilised life, the natives thus merited the attention and protection of the Church. In the writings of Bernardino de Sahagún, Juan de Torquemada, Bartolomé de las Casas and other sixteenth-century friars one can frequently discern admiration for the complexity and sophistication of pre-Hispanic civilisation. Of course, not all aspects of native culture were appreciated, and native religion in particular was considered evil and barbaric, anathema to successful conversion and the construction of the new utopian world.

Of the religious orders in sixteenth-century Mexico, or New Spain as it was then called, the Franciscans were the most prolific recorders of native

19

customs and beliefs. The acknowledged favourites of both the Spanish Crown and Hernán Cortés, the Franciscans founded the first mission in Mexico City in 1524. Like the other religious orders, the Franciscans sought the true conversion of the natives, something that could not be achieved without a thorough knowledge of their language, customs and beliefs. Among the first successfully to study Aztec language and culture was Fray Andrés de Olmos, and he is probably the author of one of the most important accounts of Aztec creation mythology, the *Historia de los mexicanos por sus pinturas*. Still another major mythological source, the *Histoyre du Mechique*, a French copy of a lost Spanish original, may derive at least in part from the work of Olmos.

By far the most renowned chronicler of Aztec society and religion was Fray Bernardino de Sahagún. Arriving in Mexico in 1529, Sahagún devoted most of his life to the study of Aztec language and culture. Like his contemporaries, he considered many Aztec traditions evil and pernicious. In an oft-cited passage, Sahagún compares himself to a physician who must understand the origins and symptoms of a disease in order to effect a cure. However, he also wanted to record a fascinating, unique world that was rapidly disintegrating before his eyes. Along with other chroniclers of his time, Sahagún not only had access to learned old men who had spent much of their lives in pre-Hispanic Aztec society, but with the assistance of native scholars he was able to consult ancient codices. Sahagún describes with some admiration these books and their relevance for his studies:

The books they had about them were painted with figures and images in such a way that they knew and had memory of the things their ancestors had done and had left in their annals, more than a thousand years back before the arrival of the Spanish in this land.

Most of these books and writings were burned at the time of the destruction of the other idolatries, but many hidden ones which we have now seen did survive and are still kept, from which we have understood their antiquities.

Although Sahagún was a prolific scholar with many contributions to his name, his most important surviving work is the *Historia general de las cosas de Nueva España*. A massive encyclopaedia of Aztec culture accompanied by more than 1850 illustrations, this is the most comprehensive and detailed treatise on any pre-Hispanic culture. Written in both Nahuatl and Spanish, the bilingual text is composed of twelve books, each with a particular subject matter. For the study of Aztec mythology, three books are of special importance. Book One provides detailed descriptions and illustrations of the major gods, while Book Three contains some of the more important myths, including the birth of Huitzilopochtli, and the quasi-historical account of Quetzalcoatl at Tula. Although Book Three contains a tangential reference to the creation of the sun at Teotihuacan, this is described in far greater detail in Book Seven, which describes celestial phenomena and the celebrations pertaining to the end of the fifty-two-year cycle.

Not everyone in New Spain applauded the work of Sahagún. By the 1570s a growing anti-native attitude was shared by both the crown and the Franciscans. The great experiment had failed; there was no New World utopia. The native populations were being decimated by disease, forced labour and over-taxation. At least as disturbing were the growing indications that true conversion was not being achieved, and that many were returning to their idolatrous ways, often with unholy blendings of Catholic and native beliefs. In this light, religious works written in native languages were increasingly considered threats to conversion and even political stability. In 1577, Philip II presented a royal decree to confiscate the bilingual works of Sahagún. Although the first version of the *Historia general* was lost, a second copy was sent to Spain in late 1579 or early 1580. It is doubtful that Sahagún ever knew what became of his life's work,

Tezcatlipoca deity impersonator to be sacrificed during the twenty-day month of Toxcatl. Illustration from Book Two of the Florentine Codex, early colonial period.

which was suppressed and forgotten until its rediscovery in 1779. Now commonly known as the Florentine Codex, this manuscript is in the Mediceo-Laurentian Library in Florence.

Aside from the Florentine Codex there are many other central Mexican pictorial manuscripts created under Spanish patronage, and quite frequently these books were illustrated by artists familiar with pre-Hispanic conventions. The magnificent Codex Borbonicus, rendered in almost pure Aztec style, was probably painted shortly after the Spanish conquest, possibly as a guide to native calendrics and religion. Along with providing important texts describing native gods and ritual, such manuscripts as the Magliabechiano, Telleriano-Remensis and Vaticanus A codices also present detailed illustrations of costume and other attributes of major Aztec gods. The Vaticanus A, also known as the Codex Ríos, contains a unique section illustrating the levels of the sky and underworld, a version of the five suns myth, and the mythical battle between Quetzalcoatl and Tezcatlipoca at Tollan.

Although containing little illustrative material, the closest surviving equivalent to the Florentine Codex in the Maya region is the *Relación de las cosas de Yucatan*. Written by the Franciscan Fray Diego de Landa about 1566, this study also offers an encyclopaedic survey of native culture, in this case the lowland Maya of Yucatan. However, in terms of quality, content and scope this manuscript in no way approaches the work of Sahagún. A self-acknowledged book burner, Landa wrote his *Relación* in Spain during his trial for instigating the notorious 1562 *auto de fé* at Mani, during which thousands of Yucatec Maya were tortured under suspicion of idolatry. Clearly, Landa was no unbiased or sympathetic chronicler of native traditions. Although he provides valuable information concerning Yucatec Maya history, calendrics and ritual, there is virtually no reference to Maya mythology. The only noteworthy exception is a somewhat garbled reference to the flood. Unlike those of central Mexico, there are no major extant colonial Spanish texts devoted to Maya mythology.

For the Maya region, the important colonial mythological sources were written by the Maya themselves. As an aid to conversion in New Spain, the religious orders adapted the Latin alphabet to record native languages. Almost all of the god names and sacred places mentioned in this book derive from these colonial spellings. The alphabetical systems were frequently taught to youths culled from the native élite, who would then serve as teachers of church doctrine. However, it was not long before native people were recording their own traditions with the new Latin-based orthographies (spelling systems). Such is the case for the most outstanding document of Maya religion known, the *Popol Vuh* of the Quiché of highland Guatemala. For sixteenth-century central Mexico, no extant mythological account approaches the *Popol Vuh* in either complexity or scope. The original manuscript, now lost, was evidently transcribed into colonial Quiché spelling during the later half of the sixteenth century. The *Popol Vuh* probably derived from a pre-Hispanic book or series of books, augmented by Quiché oral traditions. The surviving copy of the *Popol Vuh* derives from the work of the Dominican Fray Francisco Ximénez, who between 1701 and 1703 copied and translated the manuscript into Spanish while in his parish town of Chichicastenango. Ximénez graphically describes his efforts at recording ancient Quichean culture:

It was with great reserve that these manuscripts were kept among them, with such secrecy, that neither the ancient ministers knew of it, and investigating this point, while I was in the parish of Santo Tomás Chichicastenango, I found that it was the doctrine which they first imbibed with their mother's milk, and that all of them knew of it almost by heart, and I found that they had many of these books among them.

The original Ximénez transcription and accompanying Spanish translation is now housed in the Newberry Library in Chicago.

The *Popol Vuh* is thematically divided into three major sections: the first concerns the primordial origins of the world: the second, the mythical doings of

Market day at Chichicastenango, Guatemala. In the background is the church of Santo Tomás, the parish church of Francisco Ximénez, the Dominican scholar who copied and translated the Popol Vuh.

two sets of twins and the origins of modern humans and maize; and the third, the legendary history of the Quiché, ending with a list of kings extending to 1550. The following discussion of Maya mythology describes major episodes from the first and especially second sections. In recent years, it has become increasingly apparent that the *Popol Vuh* episode of the hero twins and their descent to the underworld was present among the Classic Maya, well over six hundred years before the Spanish conquest. Thus the *Popol Vuh* serves as an essential document for understanding not only the Postclassic Quiché, but Classic Maya religion as well.

Aside from the Quichean *Popol Vuh* of highland Guatemala, another major body of early Maya mythology is known for the lowland Maya of the Yucatan Peninsula. Like their Quichean contemporaries, the colonial Yucatec Maya also began recording their traditions in a Latin-based alphabet. The most important corpus of native writings survives in a series of community books named after the native priest Chilam Balam, who prophesied the coming of the Spanish. Along with the name of the ancient prophet, each book is called by the town from which it derives. Among the most famous of these manuscripts are the Book of the Chilam Balam of Chumayel and the Book of the Chilam Balam of Tizimin, both bearing the names of communities which still exist in Yucatan.

To this day, forms of the Chilam Balam books are still being written by traditional scribes in remote communities of Quintana Roo in Mexico.

Although none of the colonial Chilam Balam manuscripts predate the eighteenth century, they often contain references to ancient myth and history probably copied from earlier colonial texts and still older screenfold books. A great many of the texts describe auguries concerned with repeating cycles of time. The repetitive nature of these cycles frequently makes for a telescoping or overlapping of time, so that a single passage can contain events pertaining to colonial, pre-Hispanic and even mythical eras. Given the strongly divinatory nature of many of these texts, it is not surprising that they are often arcane and difficult to interpret. None the less, three of the texts, found in the community books of Chumayel, Tizimin and Mani, share closely related accounts of the mythical flood and the re-creation of the world.

The early colonial Aztec also continued to create books for their own uses. Don Baltasar, a native leader of Culhuacan, was tried in 1539 for hiring a native artist to illustrate his genealogy, beginning with the emergence of his ancestors and certain gods from a sacred cave. Although this seems to have been primarily a pictorial document, the Aztec also composed Nahuatl accounts written in the new Latin-based spelling. This may have been the case with the remarkable document known as the *Leyenda de los soles*. Writing in a formal and archaic Nahuatl, the author seems to have been an Aztec trained by Franciscan schooling. Like the *Historia de los mexicanos por sus pinturas* and the *Popol Vuh*, this manuscript was probably transcribed from one or several pre-Hispanic documents. After narrating the origins of the world, people and maize, the account continues with the legend of Quetzalcoatl and Tollan, and ends with actual Aztec history. Since the final historical section is incomplete, it is unknown whether the document ended with early colonial genealogies. As in the *Popol Vuh*, the linking of such genealogies to myth was commonly used to validate lineages and ancestral rights.

The colonial recording and documentation of native traditions diminished rapidly after the sixteenth century. Many of the manuscripts mentioned were either forgotten or suppressed, and not until the mid-eighteenth century was there a renewed interest in native customs and beliefs, beginning an important period for the rediscovery of pre-Hispanic and early colonial manuscripts. The Italian Lorenzo Boturini journeyed through Mexico amassing a major collection of pre-Hispanic and sixteenth-century documents. In 1744, Spanish colonial authorities expelled Boturini and confiscated his library. Although Boturini was eventually exonerated of all charges in Spain, his precious collection remained in Mexico where it was eventually dismantled.

Following the independence of Mexico and Guatemala from Spain in the early nineteenth century, the search for manuscripts continued at an even more vigorous pace. While in Mexico from 1830 to 1840, the French physicist J. M. A. Aubin amassed a large number of early documents, many from the former Boturini collection. Taken to France, they eventually became part of the Bibliothèque Nationale in Paris. But another Frenchman, the eccentric Abbé

Charles Etienne Brasseur de Bourbourg, ranks as the most famous discoverer of colonial manuscripts. With his clerical title and charming manner, Brasseur de Bourbourg gained access to many unpublished manuscripts in Mexico, Guatemala and Spain. Although Carl Scherzer first published a Spanish version of the *Popol Vuh* in 1857, this was soon eclipsed by the 1861 Brasseur de Bourbourg edition in Quiché and French. In fact, the now widely used title *Popol Vuh* derives from the French edition. While in Spain in 1863, Brasseur de Bourbourg had the good fortune to discover the *Relación de las cosas de Yucatan* by Diego de Landa. A few years later, in 1866, he also found a major portion of the pre-Hispanic Maya Codex Madrid. Although Brasseur de Bourbourg was himself most proud of discovering the Codex Chimalpopoca, which contains the *Leyenda de los soles*, this work was previously part of the Boturini collection and had already been copied and translated by Aubin.

Brasseur de Bourbourg has been justly praised for his tireless efforts in searching out rare manuscripts, but his often fanciful interpretations were poorly received by his contemporaries and subsequent researchers. He was convinced that the pre-Hispanic and colonial documents contained hidden references to Atlantis and cataclysmic geological events. The noted nineteenth century linguist Daniel Garrison Brinton had this to say concerning the abbé's commentary to the Troano fragment of the Codex Madrid:

It is painful not to be able to say a single word in favor of his views . . . They are so utterly wild that we are almost afraid to state them.

Although few of his interpretations have stood the test of time, Brasseur de Bourbourg deserves lasting credit for calling attention to and publishing some of the major documents pertaining to ancient Mesoamerica.

The systematic publication of the screenfold books constituted another major development in nineteenth-century studies of ancient Mesoamerican religion. From 1831 to 1846 the Irishman Edward King, Viscount Kingsborough, published his famed series *Antiquities of Mexico* at a cost of £32,000. The nine massive volumes contained colour copies by the artist Agostino Aglio of codices from England and continental Europe, including the Borgia, Dresden and the Vindobonensis. For his efforts, Lord Kingsborough died of typhus in 1837 in a debtor's prison.

Along with pre-Hispanic and colonial manuscripts, ancient sculpture and ceramics are major sources for interpreting Aztec and Maya mythology. In the early colonial period of the sixteenth century, pre-Hispanic stone sculptures were considered potent satanic threats to successful conversion. Writing in 1531, the bishop of New Spain, Juan de Zumárraga, reported destroying 20,000 idols. None the less, many sculptures survived, whether hidden in caves, on mountain tops, or even buried under the foundations of Mexico City. In 1790 two major monuments were discovered buried in the central plaza of Mexico City. After over 250 years of conversion and colonial rule, these monuments were no longer viewed as a threat. Rather than being destroyed, the newly discovered Calendar Stone and Coatlicue sculptures were treated as objects of

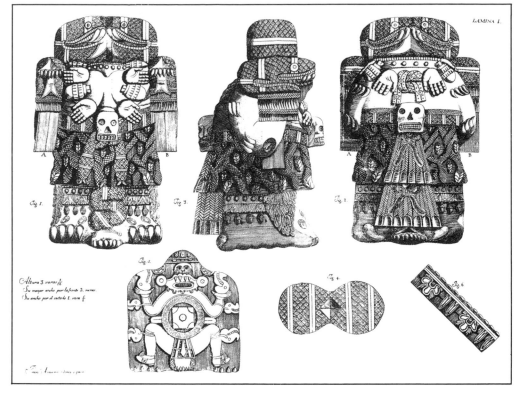

Illustration of the Coatlicue sculpture by León y Gama, first published in 1792.

curiosity and study. In 1792 Antonio de León y Gama published a detailed analysis of the two monuments, both now cornerstones of the Museo Nacional de Antropología in Mexico City.

In the Maya region, the most prolific period for the creation of monuments was not at the time of the Spanish conquest but long before, during the Classic period. The great majority of Classic Maya cities lay abandoned in forest bush, far from centres of colonial occupation. For this reason, they were largely ignored until active exploration developed near the end of the colonial period. In 1784 José Antonio Calderón reported on the Classic site of Palenque, which was subsequently visited by Antonio del Río, Guillermo Dupaix and other late colonial explorers. However, it was John Lloyd Stephens and Frederick Catherwood who first brought worldwide attention to Classic Maya antiquities. Between 1839 and 1842 Stephens and Catherwood traversed much of the Maya region and published two accounts of their journeys. Combining the engaging and vivid accounts written by Stephens and the fine illustrations of Catherwood, the volumes were extremely popular and gave rise to a future generation of explorers and researchers.

For the later half of the nineteenth century, Alfred P. Maudslay and Teobert Maler deserve special mention for their efforts in discovering and recording Maya monuments. A century later, the publications of Maudslay and

Maler continue to be indispensable sources for the study of Maya writing and religion. Inspired by the writings of Stephens, the Englishman Alfred Maudslay first visited the Maya region in 1881. During the ensuing years until 1894, Maudslay travelled to Copan, Quirigua, Palenque, Chichen Itza and other Maya sites, recording stone monuments with photographs and plaster casts. Publication of his photographs with fine drawings by Annie Hunter began in 1889, and the final work appeared in 1902 under the title *Archaeology: Biologia Centrali-Americana*. Teobert Maler, a naturalised Austrian citizen, first came to Mexico in 1865 as a soldier in the army of the ill-fated emperor Maximilian. Beginning in the 1880s, Maler recorded Maya ruins and sculpture with notes, figures, maps and, most notably, excellent photographs, labouring for months at a time through thorny brush and jungle under the most trying and difficult conditions. The only institutional support he received was from the Peabody Museum of Harvard University, which from 1901 to 1911 published a series of monographs describing his explorations in the southern Maya lowlands. Unfortunately, much of Maler's work never has been published. He died in 1917, angry, embittered and largely ignored by the new generation of Maya scholars.

With the publication of stone monuments and other remains, late-nineteenth-century scholars began to incorporate archaeological finds into the study of pre-Hispanic codices and colonial texts. Among the most brilliant was Ernst Förstemann, then chief librarian of the Royal Public Library at Dresden and caretaker of the Maya Codex Dresden. His ground-breaking research on this codex and other manuscripts provided fundamental insights into the nature of ancient Maya calendrics, mathematics and writing, including the all-important base date of 4 Ahau 8 Cumku for the great Maya Long Count, clearly an event of vast mythological importance for the ancient Maya. Förstemann's pioneering work made it possible for Joseph Goodman and others to determine the base date of 3114 BC for the present Long Count cycle. The delineation of the Long Count system also demonstrated that the majority of Maya sites and monuments dated well before the Late Postclassic period of Spanish contact.

A contemporary of Förstemann, Eduard Georg Seler was born in 1849 in what was then Prussia. Seler was one of the most brilliant and prolific scholars to work with the manuscripts and art of ancient Mexico. Along with an encyclopaedic understanding of native sources and culture, Seler possessed a keen visual eye and made many important identifications in the ancient codices and sculpture. Although Seler worked successfully with ancient Maya religion and art, he is best known for his studies of central Mexican codices, most notably the Borgia Group. Seler was generously assisted in his research by the wealthy American Joseph Florimond, who bore the papal title of Duc du Loubat. Wishing to finance not only the publication of accurate facsimiles of ancient and early colonial pictorial manuscripts but also their interpretation, Florimond founded a chair for Seler at the University of Berlin in 1899. Thanks to his support, Seler published major commentaries to four screenfold codices, the Aubin Tonalamatl, the Fejérváry-Mayer, the Vaticanus B and finally the Codex

Borgia, the last and greatest of the Seler commentaries. Many of Seler's articles appear in his five-volume collected works, the *Gesammelte Abhandlungen zur Amerikanischen Sprach-und Altertumskunde.*

The late nineteenth- and early twentieth-century regime of Porfirio Diaz marked an important period for the study of Aztec language and culture in Mexico. Many carefully edited and sumptuous volumes pertaining to Aztec history and culture derive from this epoch, including the many works of Joaquín García Icazbalceta. One of the most renowned Mexican scholars was Francisco del Paso y Troncoso, a skilled translator of Classical Nahuatl who published many important texts on Aztec religion. In 1899 he produced a facsimile edition and commentary to the most important Aztec screenfold, the Codex Borbonicus. But his major interest was the massive corpus of Sahaguntine material. Paso y Troncoso scoured the libraries of Europe in search of sixteenth-century Aztec documents. He worked in Madrid and Florence from 1892 to 1916, never once returning to Mexico. Unfortunately, a combination of factors, including the Mexican Revolution, First World War, and his own compulsive insistence on detailed notes, prevented much of his work from being adequately published.

The study of Aztec religion continued to thrive during the first half of the twentieth century, with former Seler students among the more prominent scholars, including Walter Lehmann and Walter Krickeberg. Another German, Hermann Beyer, was also strongly influenced by the approach and findings of Seler. One of Beyer's students was the Mexican Alfonso Caso, one of the greatest Mesoamerican archaeologists of the twentieth century and an expert in highland Mexican writing, calendrics and religion.

By the end of the Porfiriato, archaeological excavations were underway in many areas of Mexico. Some of the first controlled excavations in Mexico were begun in 1909 by Manuel Gamio, a student of the famed American anthropologist Franz Boas. In 1922 Gamio published a massive work on the site and present community of Teotihuacan, including his excavations at the famed Temple of Quetzalcoatl. However, the chronological relationship of the Aztecs, Toltecs and Teotihuacan was still poorly understood, and for many years Teotihuacan was considered the great Tollan of Aztec legend. In 1941 the ethnohistorian Wigberto Jiménez Moreno established that Tula was the real Tollan of the Toltecs, and it then became possible to determine the development of central Mexican culture from Teotihuacan to Tula and finally to the Aztecs.

In 1978 a massive stone monument was discovered in Mexico City at the heart of the former Aztec capital of Tenochtitlan. A representation of the slain goddess Coyolxauhqui, this monument marked the base of the most sacred Aztec structure, the great Templo Mayor, situated at the symbolic hub of the Aztec universe. From 1978 to 1982, excavations directed by Eduardo Matos Moctezuma uncovered the foundations of the Templo Mayor. The sculpture and many rich offerings found in the excavations confirmed colonial accounts that the north side of the dual temple structure was dedicated to Tlaloc, the god of rain and lightning, while the southern temple marked the shrine of Huitzilopochtli, the cult god of the Aztec. Whereas the Tlaloc half symbolised a watery mountain of sustenance, the southern half represented Coatepec, the mountain where the newly born Huitzilopochtli slew Coyolxauhqui and her four hundred brothers. In all of Mesoamerica, no archaeological project has pertained so directly to known native mythology. The Templo Mayor project constituted the dramatic excavation of Aztec myth as well as of artefacts.

During the first half of the twentieth century, the Carnegie Institution of Washington played a prominent role in Maya archaeology. With its support, major investigations were performed at Kaminaljuyu, Uaxactun, Chichen Itza and other sites in the Maya region. Sir J. Eric S. Thompson was among the prominent archaeologists affiliated with the Carnegie Institution, and for much of this century he dominated the fields of ancient Maya writing and religion. Like Seler, Thompson used his extensive knowledge of central Mexican religion to interpret Maya writing and art, and recognised the importance of recent Maya ethnography for studying pre-Hispanic Maya religion.

In their decipherment of Maya hieroglyphic writing, Thompson and his contemporaries relied heavily on the epigraphic insights of Ernst Förstemann. Ancient Maya writing was thought to deal primarily with calendrics and astronomical lore, with little concern for historical or mythological events. However, this view changed dramatically in the early 1960s with epigraphic breakthroughs by Heinrich Berlin and Tatiana Proskouriakoff, who established that Classic Maya script was not just calendrical but contained historical references to birth, accession, marriage, warfare and other human events. These episodes were not limited to humans but were also recorded for the gods in distant antiquity.

At about the same time as the discoveries of Berlin and Proskouriakoff, yet another fundamental change occurred in the study of Maya writing. The Russian epigrapher Yuri Knorozov had argued since the 1950s that ancient Maya writing was a phonetic syllabic script. Although Thompson was sharply critical of this phonetic approach, other scholars began expanding on the findings of Knorozov, and it is now widely recognised that Maya writing is strongly phonetic. The decipherment of Maya writing is continuing at a rapid pace, and each year there are new readings that shed more light on deity names, mythical events and other aspects of Maya religion.

Although Classic Maya monuments do contain references to gods and mythology, the most important source of Classic Maya myths appears on another medium – finely carved or painted ceramic vessels. Over the years these vessels have been found in controlled excavations of royal tombs, but by the 1960s vast numbers of Maya pots began appearing on the art market as the result of unfortunate aggressive looting. Suddenly there was a major but little understood corpus of elaborate narrative scenes. In 1973, archaeologist Michael D. Coe suggested that much of the vessel imagery concerns an ancestral version of the Quichean *Popol Vuh*, a detailed account of two sets of twins through their underworld journeys. Although there have been some minor modifications in the ensuing years, it is now clear that a form of the *Popol Vuh* creation epic

Late Classic Maya vase illustrating supernatural figures (Museum of Mankind, London), c. 7th century AD.

was present among the Classic Maya, with many episodes appearing on contemporaneous Maya vases.

Thanks to Sahagún and other sixteenth-century chroniclers we have excellent documentation of Aztec myth and ritual, and quite frequently a single myth can be found in several sources. The central Mexican material has also been studied intensively by trained Aztec specialists for over a century in a tradition that continues unabated to this day. However, the study of ancient Maya mythology is still in its infancy. Aside from the *Popol Vuh* there are relatively few contact-period texts pertaining to Maya myths. Moreover, ancient Maya writing and art are still being deciphered, and new texts and scenes continue to be discovered at a rapid pace. However, even at this stage of research, pre-Hispanic Maya texts and art can tell us a great deal about ancient Maya mythology, including myths not documented in the colonial record. The intricate, highly developed nature of Classic Maya writing and iconography provides us with a unique opportunity to see into a religious world some thousand years before Spanish contact.

Aztec mythology

In 1524, a scant three years after the conquest of Mexico, a group of Aztec scholars spoke with the first Franciscan missionaries to arrive in the newly founded capital of Mexico City. These were some of the words spoken by the Aztec in defence of their beliefs:

You said that we know not the Lord of the Close Vicinity, to Whom the heavens and earth belong. You said that our gods are not true gods. New words are these that you speak; because of them we are disturbed, because of them we are troubled. For our ancestors before us, who lived upon the earth, were unaccustomed to speak thus. From them we have inherited our pattern of life which in truth did they hold; in reverence they held, they honoured our gods.

This remarkable dialogue, recorded in the works of Fray Bernardino de Sahagún, marks an initial exchange between two worlds of religious thought that had developed entirely independently of one another for thousands of years.

To the Aztec, creation is the result of complementary opposition and conflict. Much like a dialogue between two individuals, the interaction and exchange between opposites constitute a creative act. The concept of interdependent opposition is embodied in the great creator god, **Ometeotl**, God of Duality, who resides in the uppermost thirteenth heaven of Omeyocan, Place of Duality. Possessing both the male and female creative principles, Ometeotl was also referred to as the couple **Tonacatecuhtli** and **Tonacacihuatl**, Lord and Lady of Our Sustenance. Although Ometeotl constitutes the ultimate source of all, his and her progeny of lesser but still powerful deities perform the actual deeds of creation. Since humans are the products or offspring of these younger gods, Ometeotl is something akin to our grandparents. Perhaps for this reason, and to indicate his and her primordial origins, Ometeotl is often portrayed as an aged being with a sagging lower jaw. However, old age is by no means synonymous with infirmity; among the Aztec and other Mesoamerican peoples, individuals are thought to accrue more life force in the process of ageing.

Two children of Ometeotl, **Quetzalcoatl** and **Tezcatlipoca**, play a very special role in Aztec creation mythology. Sometimes allies and sometimes adversaries, these two gods create the heavens and earth. Quetzalcoatl, the plumed serpent, is widely identified with water, fertility and, by extension, life itself. One aspect of Quetzalcoatl, Ehecatl, is the god of wind, who appears in the breath of living beings and the breezes that bring the fructifying rain clouds. Whereas Quetzalcoatl is widely portrayed as a benevolent culture hero identified with balance, harmony and life, Tezcatlipoca represents conflict and

Quetzalcoatl, the plumed serpent. The feathered body of the serpent undulates down the back (right). The human face of Quetzalcoatl projects out of a rayed solar ring (left), and it is possible that he is here portrayed as the sun of wind, or Nahui Ehecatl, the second creation in the Aztec cosmogony. Aztec stone sculpture (Museum of Mankind, London), Late Postclassic period.

change. Among the many Aztec epithets for this awesome being are 'the adversary' and 'he whose slaves we are'. The name Tezcatlipoca signifies Smoking Mirror, and this god typically appears with a smoking obsidian mirror at the back of his head and another replacing one of his feet. The smoking quality of the mirror may allude to the black obsidian glass, but it also evokes his mysterious nature, constantly changing through a cloud-like haze.

A great many other deities inhabit the Aztec pantheon, among them gods and goddesses of agriculture and rain, fire, love and pleasure, death, war and celestial bodies. A large number were worshipped over much of Late Postclassic central Mexico, and not only do they appear in Aztec manuscripts and sculpture, but also in the five pre-Hispanic books comprising the Borgia Group. The virtually ubiquitous **Tlaloc**, god of rain and lightning, can be traced back as early as the first century BC in central Mexico. In the Late Postclassic period he typically appears with goggles and a pronounced upper lip containing a set of large, jaguar-like teeth. His consort **Chalchiuhtlicue**, She of the Jade Skirt, is the water goddess of rivers and standing water. The youthful maize god, **Cinteotl**, often displays a broken line running down his face, and maize ears in his headdress. One of the more striking fertility deities is **Xipe Totec**, a deity of springtime rejuvenation and the patron of goldsmiths. He can be readily identified by his mask and suit of flayed human skin. During the Aztec twenty-day month of Tlacaxipehualiztli, men impersonated Xipe Totec by wearing the skins of sacrificial victims. The significance of this is obscure, although some interpret the skin as new spring growth covering the earth.

A number of deities concern fire, of whom the most ancient is **Huehueteotl**, the Old God; he is portrayed on incense burners as early as 500 BC in Puebla. Another important fire deity is **Xiuhtecuhtli**, the Turquoise Lord, god of time and a patron god of rulership.

Other central Mexican gods personify pleasure and lust. **Xochipilli**, the Flower Prince, overlaps considerably with the corn god, and is the patron god of pleasure and the arts. Xochipilli is also closely associated with **Macuilxochitl**, Five Flower, a god of games and gambling. The lovely goddess **Xochiquetzal**, or Flower Quetzal, is frequently distinguished by her flowery headband containing two horn-like tufts of plumes from the emerald quetzal bird. She is a goddess of the arts, physical pleasure and amorous love. The goddess **Tlazolteotl**, Filth Goddess, is associated with the consequences of lust and licentiousness. Another of her names, Tlaelquani, Eater of Excrement, expresses her identification with confession and purification; the blackened region around her mouth probably refers to this unpleasant but necessary duty. The primary god of death was **Mictlantecuhtli**, Lord of Mictlan, the dark and gloomy underworld. Frequently accompanied by his wife, **Mictlancihuatl**, he is depicted as a skeleton wearing a pleated conical cap and other vestments of paper.

A great many central Mexican gods represented the sun, the planet Venus, stars, the Milky Way galaxy and other celestial bodies. Perhaps because their permutations through the sky were viewed as cosmic battles, many were identified with war. One of the fiercest of these celestial gods was **Tlahuizcalpantecuhtli**, Lord of the Dawn, the personification of Venus as Morning Star. The first appearance of Venus as Morning Star was greatly feared in ancient Mesoamerica, since it was believed that its light could inflict great injury. Several codices in the Borgia Group contain complex astronomical tables predicting the cycles of Venus over a span of roughly 104 years. In these scenes, Tlahuizcalpantecuhtli hurls his fiery rays with a spear-thrower. **Mixcoatl**, Cloud Serpent, was another stellar god. His body is usually painted with the red and white stripes associated with captive warriors destined for sacrifice. A god of the Milky Way, Mixcoatl personified the souls of warriors that became stars at death. Among the most prominent of the sky gods is **Tonatiuh**, the sun. First known in the art of the Early Postclassic Toltec, Tonatiuh commonly appears as a weapon-wielding warrior within a rayed solar disc. Although central to the cult of war – much of its underlying ethos was to obtain captives and hearts for the sun – Tonatiuh was not the only Aztec solar war god.

The creation of heaven and earth

Like the Maya and other Mesoamerican peoples, the Aztec believed that other worlds existed before our own. According to the Aztec, there were four previous worlds or 'suns', each named by a date in the 260-day cycle and identified with a particular deity and race of humans. Along with its calendrical name, each sun was linked with earth, wind, fire or water. Each of the four elements relates not only to the nature and composition of its world, but also to its destruction. Thus, for example, the sun of earth, Nahui Ocelotl (4 Jaguar), is destroyed by jaguars, creatures closely identified with the earth and the underworld. Tezcatlipoca and Quetzalcoatl figure prominently in the four suns, as if the multiple creations and destructions are the result of cosmic battle between these two great adversaries. In addition to its representations in ancient Aztec sculpture, more than ten versions of this myth appear in colonial sources. Although the colonial documents are not consistent in the order of the various suns, two of the earliest and most important sources, the *Historia de los mexicanos por sus pinturas* and the *Leyenda de los soles*, share the same order as appears on Aztec monuments. The following version derives from these two major accounts.

Within the thirteenth heaven, the creator couple give birth to four sons. The first is the Red Tezcatlipoca, but it is the second son, the Black Tezcatlipoca, who corresponds to the Tezcatlipoca so prominent in Aztec myth. The third son is Quetzalcoatl and the fourth, Huitzilopochtli, is the patron god of the Aztecs. Together these four brothers make fire, the heavens, earth, sea and underworld, the first human couple, and the sacred calendar. The Black Tezcatlipoca rules over the first world, the sun of earth, peopled by a race of giants. So powerful are these giants that they pull up trees with their bare hands. Wielding a staff, Quetzalcoatl strikes Tezcatlipoca into the sea. Rising out of the ocean, he becomes a great jaguar, still seen today as the constellation Ursa Major, and with his return the race of giants is utterly devoured by fierce jaguars. One early source suggests that the Aztec considered the fossil remains of extinct mammoth and other great creatures found near Tenochtitlan as the bones of this ancient race.

Quetzalcoatl presides over the next creation, the sun of wind. This world is destroyed by Tezcatlipoca, who bests Quetzalcoatl by kicking him down. As a result, Quetzalcoatl and his race of people are carried off by fierce winds. The descendants of this early race can be seen as monkeys who swing and scamper high up in the forest trees. The *Leyenda de los soles* describes this world as follows:

This Sun is known as 4-Wind.
Those who lived under this second Sun were carried away by the wind. It was under the Sun 4-Wind that they all disappeared.
They were carried away by the wind. They became monkeys.
Their homes, their trees – everything was taken away by the wind.
And this sun itself was also swept away by the wind.

The rain god Tlaloc rules over the third creation, the sun of rain. This world is destroyed by Quetzalcoatl in a rain of fire – probably volcanic ash, a relatively common geological occurrence in central Mexico. The fiery rain magically transforms the people of this race into turkeys. The fourth sun, the sun of water, is presided over by the wife of Tlaloc, Chalchiuhtlicue, She of the Jade Skirt, the goddess of streams and standing water. A great flood destroys

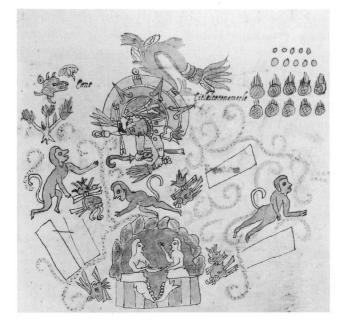

The destruction of the sun of wind and the transformation of humans into monkeys. In the upper portion of the scene, Quetzalcoatl appears as the sun of wind encircled by a rayed solar sign. Codex Vaticanus A, f. 6r (detail), early colonial period.

BELOW *Chalchiuhtlicue, the Aztec goddess of standing water and the sun of water, Nahui Atl. Codex Borbonicus, p 5 (detail), early colonial Aztec.*

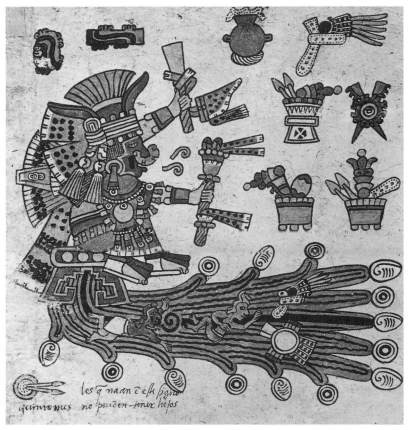

this world, and its people are transformed into fish. So massive is the flood that the mountains are washed away, causing the heavens to crash down upon the earth.

The *Leyenda de los soles* mentions a man, Tata, and his wife Nene, who are cared for by Tezcatlipoca. Much like a New World form of Noah and his wife, they escape the flood by hiding in a hollow tree. Told by Tezcatlipoca to eat only one ear of maize apiece, they slowly nibble the grains of corn and watch the waters gradually recede. When it is finally safe to leave the tree, they see a fish – one of their unfortunate brethren, transformed by the deluge. Tempted by the promise of ready food, they create new fire with a fire drill and cook the fish. But the star gods Citlallinicue and Citlallatonac notice the smoke and call out: 'Gods, who has made fire? Who has smoked the heavens?' Immediately Tezcatlipoca descends from the sky and in a fury asks, 'What have you done, Tata? What have you all done?' In an instant he cuts off their heads and places them on their buttocks: thus were the first dogs created.

The restoration of the sky and earth

Although clearly agents in the destruction of the previous four suns, Tezcatlipoca and Quetzalcoatl are also credited with the re-creation of the heavens and earth, not as adversaries, but as allies. The *Historia de los mexicanos por sus pinturas* relates one important version in which, aided by four other deities, the four sons of the creator couple create four roads leading to the centre of the earth. With the earth thus divided into four quadrants, the eight gods raise the heavens. To help support and sustain the sky, Tezcatlipoca and Quetzalcoatl transform themselves into two enormous trees. The tree of Tezcatlipoca is marked by shining mirrors, and that of Quetzalcoatl by the plumes of the emerald quetzal bird. To reward them for their efforts, Tonacatecuhtli makes them lords of the heavens and stars; the Milky Way is their road by which they cross the starry sky.

The Aztec earth deity, Tlaltecuhtli. Detail from stone sculpture, Late Postclassic period.

In another Aztec myth of creation, Quetzalcoatl and Tezcatlipoca fashion the heavens and earth by dismembering the great earth monster, Tlaltecuhtli. Although the name Tlaltecuhtli means Earth Lord, this being is actually dually sexed and is often described as female. Tlaltecuhtli sometimes merges with another earth monster, a great caiman whose spiny crocodilian back forms the mountain ridges of the world. The Tlaltecuhtli myth was widespread in Meso-america, and a form was present among the Maya of Yucatan.

In one Aztec version appearing in the *Histoyre du Mechique*, Quetzalcoatl and Tezcatlipoca descend from the sky to observe Tlaltecuhtli striding upon the sea. So fierce is her desire for flesh that not only does she have a great toothy maw, but also gnashing mouths at her elbows, knees and other joints. Quetzalcoatl and Tezcatlipoca agree that creation cannot be completed with such a horrendous beast in their midst. To create the earth, therefore, Quetzalcoatl and Tezcatlipoca transform themselves into two great serpents. One snake seizes the left hand and right foot of Tlaltecuhtli and the other her right hand and left foot, and between them they tear the monster apart. The upper portion of her body then becomes the earth, while the other half is thrown into the sky to create the heavens.

The violent slaying and dismemberment of Tlaltecuhtli angers the other gods. To console the mutilated earth, they decree that all plants needed for human life will derive from her body. From her hair are fashioned trees, flowers and herbs, and from her skin come the grasses and smaller flowers. Her eyes are the source of wells, springs and small caves; her mouth, great rivers and caverns; and her nose, mountain ridges and valleys. At times, the earth goddess can still be heard screaming in the night for the blood and hearts of people. Ultimately, only sacrificial flesh and blood can soothe and quiet Tlaltecuhtli sufficiently to keep her producing the fruits needed for human life.

The origin of people

The gods decide, having refashioned the world, that people are needed to repopulate the earth. A number of colonial accounts describe the creation of the present race of humans; the following version derives from the *Leyenda de los soles* and the *Histoyre du Mechique*. It is agreed that the god of wind, Quetzalcoatl, must go to the underworld to retrieve the human bones of the last creation, the race turned into fish by the flood. The underworld, a dangerous place known as Mictlan, is ruled by the devious skeletal god Mictlantecuhtli, Lord of Mictlan. Once in the underworld, Quetzalcoatl asks Mictlantecuhtli and his wife for the bones of the ancestors:

And then Quetzalcoatl went to Mictlan. He approached Mictlantecuhtli and Mictlan-cihuatl; at once he spoke to them:
'I come in search of the precious bones in your possession. I have come for them.'
And Mictlantecuhtli asked of him, 'What shall you do with them, Quetzalcoatl?'
And once again Quetzalcoatl said, 'The gods are anxious that someone should inhabit the earth.'

The gods of death and life, Mictlantecuhtli and Ehecatl-Quetzalcoatl. Codex Borgia, p. 56 (detail), Late Postclassic period.

The crafty god of death agrees to give up the bones, provided that Quetzalcoatl can fulfil an apparently simple task. He tells Quetzalcoatl to travel around his underworld realm four times while sounding a conch shell trumpet. However, instead of a shell trumpet, Mictlantecuhtli gives Quetzalcoatl a simple conch with no holes. Not to be outsmarted, Quetzalcoatl calls upon worms to drill holes in the shell and for bees to enter the trumpet and make it roar. (As an emblem of his powers of wind and life, Quetzalcoatl is often depicted wearing the cut conch Wind Jewel on his chest.)

Hearing the conch blast, Mictlantecuhtli first allows Quetzalcoatl to take the bones of the last creation but quickly changes his mind. However, Quetzalcoatl again outwits Mictlantecuhtli and his underworld minions, and escapes with the bones. The enraged Mictlantecuhtli then commands his followers to make a deep pit. As Quetzalcoatl runs towards it, a quail bursts out and startles him, causing him to stumble into the hole.

The pit having been made, Quetzalcoatl fell in it, he stumbled and was frightened by the quail. He fell dead and the precious bones were scattered. The quail chewed and gnawed on them.

Although Quetzalcoatl eventually revives and retrieves the bones, they are now broken, and for this reason people today are of different sizes. Having escaped the underworld, Quetzalcoatl carries the precious load to Tamoanchan, a miraculous place of origin. There the old goddess Cihuacoatl, or Woman Serpent, grinds the bones into a flour-like meal which she places in a special ceramic container. The gods gather around this vessel and shed drops of their blood upon the ground bones, and from the bones of the fish people mixed with the penitential blood of the gods, the present race of humans are born.

The origin of maize

Although people thus returned to the surface of the earth, they still required food to give them sustenance and strength. While there are several distinct myths describing the origins of maize and other cultivated plants, one of the most important appears in the *Leyenda de los soles*. Versions of this myth are still known today in many regions of Mexico and Guatemala.

After creating people at Tamoanchan, all the gods go in search of their future food. Quetzalcoatl spies a red ant carrying a grain of maize, and asks him where he found this wondrous food. The ant refuses to tell, but after much bullying agrees to take Quetzalcoatl to the source, Mount Tonacatepetl, Mountain of Sustenance. Transforming himself into a black ant, Quetzalcoatl squeezes through the narrow opening and follows the red ant deep into the stony mountain to a chamber filled with seed and grain. Taking some kernels of maize, Quetzalcoatl returns to Tamoanchan. The gods chew the maize and place the mash in the mouths of the infant humans to give them strength.

They then ask, 'What are we going to do with Tonacatepetl?' Quetzalcoatl slings a rope around the mountain and tries to carry it off, but the mountain is too large to lift. Then the old diviner couple, Oxomoco and Cipactonal, cast lots to determine how to acquire the seeds of Tonacatepetl. The couple divines that the diseased god Nanahuatzin must break open the rock of sustenance, so, with the help of the four directional gods of rain and lightning, the blue, white, yellow and red Tlalocs, Nanahuatzin splits Tonacatepetl wide open, causing the maize kernels and other seeds to scatter in all directions. The Tlalocs quickly

Tlaloc pouring out water and crops from a precious jade jar. Detail of Aztec stone box (Museum of Mankind, London), Late Postclassic period.

snatch up seeds of white, black, yellow and red maize, as well as those of beans and other edible plants. Having obtained the seeds at Tonacatepetl, the Tlalocs are the real dispensers of crops as well as rain.

The origin of pulque

An alcoholic beverage made from the fermented sap of the maguey plant, pulque played a major role in Aztec ceremonial life both as a ritual drink and a sacrificial offering. Pulque was often drunk at banquets and festivals, although public intoxication was strongly condemned, particularly for those of noble birth. The mythic origins of pulque are described in one major source, the *Histoyre du Mechique*, which contains one of the few mythical references to the horrific *tzitzimime* (singular *tzitzimitl*), celestial demons of darkness that continually threaten to destroy the world. These night demons, often female, are

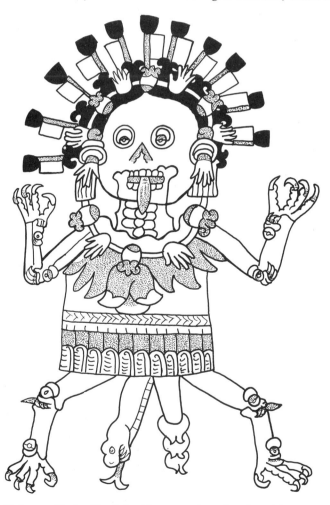

A female tzitzimitl demon. Codex Magliabechiano, p. 76r, early colonial Aztec.

the stars that do battle against the sun at every dusk and dawn.

Although humans had been provided with seeds from which to make food, there was little in their lives to inspire pleasure or joy. The gods conclude that something is needed to make people sing and dance. Quetzalcoatl decides that intoxicating drink will bring pleasure to people's lives, and he recalls Mayahuel, the lovely young goddess of maguey, who lives in the sky with her fearsome *tzitzimitl* grandmother. Finding the virgin Mayahuel asleep, Quetzalcoatl wakes her and persuades the goddess to descend with him to earth. There they join themselves into a great forked tree, with Quetzalcoatl as one branch and Mayahuel the other.

Awakening to find Mayahuel missing, the enraged grandmother calls upon her fellow *tzitzimime* star demons to find her errant granddaughter. The furious *tzitzimime* dive headlong from the sky to the tree where Quetzalcoatl and Mayahuel are hidden. Just as they arrive, the tree splits in half and the two branches crash to the ground. The grandmother *tzitzimitl* recognises the branch of Mayahuel and, savagely tearing it apart, she passes parts of her granddaughter to all the other *tzitzimime* to devour. But the branch of Quetzalcoatl is left untouched and unharmed, and once the *tzitzimime* return to the sky, Quetzalcoatl turns back into his actual form. Sadly gathering the gnawed bones of Mayahuel, Quetzalcoatl buries them in the earth, and from this simple grave grew the first maguey plant, the miraculous source of pulque.

The creation of the fifth sun

The creation of the fifth sun, Nahui Ollin, comprises the climactic end to the epic of creation. For the Aztecs, this occurred at the ancient city of Teotihuacan, located some 40 kilometres (25 miles) north-east of Mexico City, and they considered this the place where time began. The following account derives from two principal sources, the Florentine Codex and the *Leyenda de los soles*.

After the creation of the earth, people, and their food and drink, the gods convened in darkness at Teotihuacan to decide who will be the new sun to light the world:

It is told that when yet all was in darkness, when yet no sun had shone and no dawn had broken – it is said – the gods gathered themselves together and took counsel among themselves there at Teotihuacan. They spoke; they said among themselves:
   'Come hither, O gods! Who will carry the burden? Who will take it upon himself to be the sun, to bring the dawn?'

A haughty god named Tecuciztecatl quickly volunteers, but the other gods elect the humble and diseased Nanahuatzin (who had split the rock of sustenance to get maize) as a second contender. Like a warrior, he stoically accepts this as his duty and debt to the other gods. Two hills are made for Tecuciztecatl and Nanahuatzin to fast and do penance while the sacrificial pyre is prepared, and these can still be seen today as the Pyramids of the Sun and Moon. The offerings that Tecuciztecatl presents during his fast and vigil are of the finest and most costly materials. Instead of fir boughs he has quetzal plumes, and gold balls serve as his bundles of bound grass. In place of maguey spines spotted with his own blood, he offers awls of jade tipped with red coral. The incense burned by Tecuciztecatl is also of the rarest and finest quality. The offerings of Nanahuatzin, however, are of little material value. For his fir branches and grass balls he uses bundles of reeds, and he offers real maguey spines with his own blood. For his incense, he burns scabs picked from his body.

At midnight after four days of penance, the gods dress the two and whereas Tecuciztecatl is richly adorned, Nanahuatzin wears only simple vestments of paper. The gods then encircle the great sacrificial pyre, which has been burning for four days and is now fiercely hot. Standing along both sides of the fire, the gods call for Tecuciztecatl to jump into the flames. Tecuciztecatl runs towards the pyre, but the heat and searing flames terrify him and he falters. Once more he tries, and once again he is halted by the fire. Four times he runs towards the fire, but every time he wavers and stops. Finally, the gods call out for Nanahuatzin, and in an instant he runs and jumps into the fire:

And Nanahuatzin, daring all at once, determined – resolved – hardened his heart, and shut firmly his eyes. He had no fear; he did not stop short; he did not falter in fright; he did not turn back. All at once he quickly threw and cast himself into the fire; once and for all he went. Thereupon he burned; his body crackled and sizzled.

Seeing the heroic death of Nanahuatzin, Tecuciztecatl follows him into the flames and dies, and after him, the eagle and jaguar also dive into the pyre. The tips of the eagle's feathers are scorched black, and the jaguar's pelt is smudged with black spots. Because of their bravery at Teotihuacan, the eagle and jaguar became the two great military orders of Aztec warriors.

After the fiery deaths of Nanahuatzin and Tecuciztecatl, the gods wait and look to see where they might reappear. Gradually, the sky begins to redden in all directions. The gods peer and turn their heads, craning to see where brave Nanahuatzin will first emerge. Some rightly guess that Nanahuatzin will appear in the east, and pointing in that direction, they are the first to witness him emerge. No longer sickly and humble, Nanahuatzin returns rising as Tonatiuh, the fiery sun god whose rays shoot out in all directions:

And when the sun came to rise, when he burst forth, he appeared to be red; he kept swaying from side to side. It was impossible to look into his face; he blinded one with his light.

Soon after, Tecuciztecatl also rises in the east, just as brightly as Tonatiuh. So similar are the two that the other gods worry that the world will be too bright. One of the gods runs out and throws a rabbit in the face of Tecuciztecatl. Thus wounded, the face of the moon is dimmer than the sun, and during full moons, the rabbit can be seen seated in the face of the moon.

Although the sun and moon thus appear, they do not follow their paths but instead hover motionless in the sky. Tonatiuh demands the fealty and blood of the other gods before he will move. Infuriated by this arrogance, the god of the morning star known as Tlahuizcalpantecuhtli, Lord of the Dawn, shoots a dart at the sun. However, the dart misses its mark, and the sun throws his own

ABOVE *The Aztec Calendar Stone. The centre contains the date Nahui Ollin, the current sun of motion created at the site of Teotihuacan. The calendric names of the four previous creations appear within the four flanges of the Ollin sign. Aztec (Museo Nacional de Antropología, Mexico City), Late Postclassic period.*

Itztlacoliuhqui with a dart piercing his forehead. The morning star, Lord of the Dawn, is transformed into the god of stone and cold by the sun's dart. Codex Telleriano-Remensis, f. 16, early colonial Aztec.

back at the morning star, piercing Tlahuizcalpantecuhtli through the head. At this moment, the Lord of the Dawn is transformed into the god of stone and coldness, Itztlacoliuhqui, and for this reason it is always cold at the time of the dawn. The gods finally agree that they must sacrifice themselves to make the sun move. Methodically, one by one, Quetzalcoatl cuts the hearts out of each god with a sacrificial blade. The mantles and finery of the dead gods are wrapped up in sacred bundles, the form in which they are then worshipped by people. From the slaying of the gods at Teotihuacan, the Sun of Motion, Nahui Ollin, is created. Just as the gods had to sacrifice themselves, so humans must supply their own hearts and blood to ensure that the fifth sun continues to move in its path.

Mythology of the Aztec state

The Aztec myths of the five suns and of the creation of the present world, humans, maize and pulque were surely known over much of Postclassic central Mexico. Much of this mythology is very old, and probably developed out of earlier Classic period traditions. For example, a Late Classic period version of the creation of people from the remains of the last creation is represented at the Late Classic site of El Tajín, in Veracruz. In this scene, Tlaloc bleeds his member upon a dead fish-man, a reference to the race of people turned into fish by the flood.

Although the Late Postclassic creation mythology of central Mexico bears many similarities to other myths of ancient and contemporary Mesoamerica, there is another creation epic that is wholly Aztec, essentially serving as the state

Tlaloc letting blood upon a fish-man. This scene may illustrate an early version of the creation of people. Detail of bas-relief from South Ballcourt, El Tajín, Veracruz, Late Classic period.

Huitzilopochtli letting blood from his ear. A hummingbird headdress projects up from behind his right hand. Detail from colossal jaguar sculpture, Aztec (Museo Nacional de Antropología, Mexico City), Late Postclassic period.

mythology of the developing Aztec empire. This concerns the origins of **Huitzilopochtli**, Hummingbird on the Left, cult god of the Aztec people. Like the mythology that surrounds him, Huitzilopochtli seems to be an entirely Aztec innovation. Possessing attributes of Tezcatlipoca, the star god Mixcoatl and the fire god Xiuhtecuhtli, Huitzilopochtli is a solar deity whose symbolic domain overlaps considerably with that of Tonatiuh. Although of central importance to the Aztec, it is unlikely that Huitzilopochtli enjoyed a widespread and enthusiastic following outside the Valley of Mexico. Indeed, representations of him are notably rare in the art of ancient Mesoamerica.

The birth of Huitzilopochtli

Colonial accounts describing the origin of Huitzilopochtli are numerous and varied but in many versions his birth occurred at Coatepec, Serpent Mountain, a hill located near the ancient city of Tula. According to the *Historia de los mexicanos por sus pinturas* the Aztecs returned to Coatepec every year to celebrate a feast in honour of Huitzilopochtli. All the major deities in this creation epic are specific to the Aztec pantheon, and are not found among other peoples of Late Postclassic central Mexico. The mother of Huitzilopochtli, **Coatlicue**, She of the Serpent Skirt, is readily identified by her skirt of woven snakes. **Coyolxauhqui**, the half-sister of Huitzilopochtli, is partly derived from **Chantico**, an obscure central Mexican fire goddess. The name Coyolxauhqui means Painted with Bells, and she typically displays a pair of metal bells on her

Coatlicue, She of the Serpent Skirt, the mother of Huitzilopochtli. Snakes representing blood emerge from the severed stumps of her arms and throat, indicating that she has been slain. Aztec (Museo Nacional de Antropología, Mexico City), Late Postclassic period.

cheeks. She is accompanied by a multitude of brothers known as the **Centzon Huitznahua**, the Four Hundred (or innumerable) Southerners, who are thematically related to the four hundred pulque gods of Aztec belief. The most thorough accounts of the birth of Huitzilopochtli at Coatepec appear in the works of Sahagún. The following account derives from Book Three of the Florentine Codex.

One day while performing penance and sweeping at Coatepec, the chaste and pious Coatlicue discovers a ball of feathers. Wanting to save the precious feathers, Coatlicue places them in her waistband. However, when she later looks for the ball of feathers, it is gone. Unknown to her at the time, the feathers had impregnated her with the seed of Huitzilopochtli. Gradually Coatlicue grows in size until her sons, the Centzon Huitznahua, notice that she is with child.

Enraged and shamed, they furiously demand to know the father. Their elder sister, Coyolxauhqui, decides that they must slay their mother:

And their elder sister, Coyolxauhqui, said to them:
    'My elder brothers, she hath dishonored us. We can only kill our mother, the wicked one who is already with child. Who is the cause of what is in her womb?'

The news of her children's intentions terrifies the pregnant goddess, but the child within her womb consoles Coatlicue, assuring her that he is already aware and ready. Dressed in the raiment of warriors, the Centzon Huitznahua follow Coyolxauhqui to Coatepec. When her raging children reach the crest of the mountain, Coatlicue gives birth to Huitzilopochtli fully armed. Wielding his burning weapon, known as the Xiuhcoatl or Turquoise Serpent, he slays Coyolxauhqui and, cut to pieces, her body tumbles to the base of Coatepec.

Then he pierced Coyolxauhqui, and then quickly struck off her head. It stopped there at the edge of Coatepetl [Coatepec]. And her body came falling below; it fell breaking to pieces; in various places her arms, her legs, her body each fell.

Having killed Coyolxauhqui, Huitzilopochtli chases the Centzon Huitznahua around Coatepec and slays vast numbers of his half-brothers, with only a few escaping to the south.

Eduard Seler suggested at the turn of this century that the birth of Huitzilopochtli at Coatepec represents the dawning sun fighting off the gods of darkness. With his Xiuhcoatl fire serpent, Huitzilopochtli is the newly born sun shooting out burning rays and, clearly enough, the Centzon Huitznahua are the stars who at every dawn are vanquished by the rising sun. However, the precise cosmological identity of Coyolxauhqui is still unknown. Although Seler suggested that she is the moon, she bears no obvious lunar attributes, and according to Carmen Aguilera, she may represent another astronomical body of the night sky: the Milky Way.

As well as having cosmological significance, the birth of Huitzilopochtli also symbolises the Aztec ascendance over competing peoples of central Mexico. Huitzilopochtli was the supernatural embodiment of both the Aztec people and their empire. The birth of this god provided the mythic charter for

Scenes from Book Three of the Florentine Codex. The illustrations portray the birth of Huitzilopochtli (top) and the defeat of his enemies at Coatepec. Early colonial period.

the political expansion of the Aztec and their right to rule over their defeated enemies. As relative newcomers to the Valley of Mexico, the Aztecs conquered and eclipsed the existing inhabitants of the already occupied region, much as Huitzilopochtli vanquished his elder half-sister and half-brothers.

The great Templo Mayor dominated the landscape of the Aztec capital, continually reminding its citizens of Huitzilopochtli and his miraculous origins. Whereas the north side of this dual temple was dedicated to Tlaloc, the rain god, the southern half was the principal temple of Huitzilopochtli. According to native and Spanish acccounts, captive warriors were frequently sacrificed here. Stretched over a sacrificial stone, their hearts were removed and the lifeless bodies were then thrown to the base of the temple steps. Sixteenth-century sources also report that the southern side of the Templo Mayor symbolised the mythical mountain of Coatepec, the birthplace of Huitzilopochtli.

Remarkable physical proof of this appeared on 21 February 1978, when excavations by an electrical company accidently uncovered a massive stone monument of Coyolxauhqui at what was the ancient centre of Tenochtitlan. A masterful portrayal of humiliation and defeat, the monument portrays Coyolxauhqui naked and brutally dismembered. Although her head and limbs are severed from her bleeding torso, she appears in a dynamic and almost running pose, as if portrayed in the instant of tumbling down Coatepec. Excavations soon revealed that the Coyolxauhqui stone lay at the base of the stairway on the Huitzilopochtli side of the Templo Mayor. In other words, each sacrificed human prisoner thrown down the temple stairs in Aztec rituals re-enacted the killing of Coyolxauhqui at Coatepec.

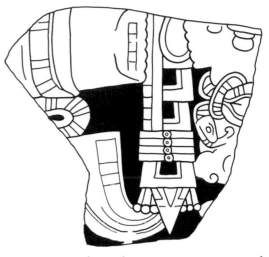

Monument fragment portraying the segmented body of the Xiuhcoatl serpent penetrating the chest of Coyolxauhqui. Aztec (Museo Templo Mayor, Mexico City), Late Postclassic period.

The Templo Mayor excavations uncovered another stone monument of Coyolxauhqui. Although fragmentary, this piece clearly portrays the Xiuhcoatl fire serpent penetrating her chest and probably illustrates the mythical origins of Aztec heart sacrifice. Just as the Xiuhcoatl serpent pierces Coyolxauhqui, the sacrificial knife would tear the heart from the human captive's chest.

Against a majestic background of aeons of world creations and cataclysmic destructions, the myth of the five suns presents sacrifice as an essential means for maintaining human life and cosmic balance. Through the penitential offering of their own blood, the gods create the present race of mankind. An even greater sacrifice occurs at Teotihuacan, where the gods slay themselves so that the sun can follow its course. In their own acts of bloodletting and sacrifice, humans are simply following a tradition set down by the gods at the time of creation. Although the five suns myth provides a rationale for some of the most important and profound rites of Postclassic central Mexico, this was not enough for the Aztec, who were interested not only in explaining their origin and role in the cosmos, but also in validating their unique status as a chosen people. For this reason, the Aztecs developed their own special mythology for their patron god Huitzilopochtli, in whose origins warfare is an explicit and central motif. The rout and utter defeat of Coyolxauhqui and the Centzon Huitznahua by Huitzilopochtli portrays in sacred myth the Aztecs' victories over their enemies, providing a mythic charter for the heart sacrifice performed on such a massive scale at the Templo Mayor.

Like the five suns episode at Teotihuacan, the vanquishing of Coyolxauhqui and her brothers describes the origins of the sun and human sacrifice. However, the Aztec imperial myth does not concern the sun god Tonatiuh, but rather the solar-related Huitzilopochtli. The fifth sun and Huitzilopochtli episodes are overlapping and probably competing myths. It is quite possible that, were it not for the Spanish conquest, the Huitzilopochtli myth might eventually have eclipscd thc solar Teotihuacan myth – much as the Aztec were increasing their domain over the peoples of ancient Mesoamerica.

Maya mythology

At the time of Spanish contact, the Maya were neither politically nor culturally a single unified people. Some thirty distinct Mayan languages were present in the sixteenth century, and most are still spoken today. The languages may be as similar as modern Spanish is to Portuguese, although the differences can also be far greater, as for example between English and French. Aside from language, there are other cultural differences between the Yucatecan Mayan speakers of the northern Maya lowlands and such highland Maya peoples as the Tzotzil, Tojolabal, Mam, Quiché, Kekchi and Chorti, who occupy the dramatic mountainous region of Chiapas, southern Guatemala and neighbouring Honduras.

In the sixteenth century, notable differences in calendrics and religion also existed between the lowland Maya of Yucatan and the Maya peoples of the southern highlands. Although an abbreviated version of the Classic Maya Long Count continued to play an essential part in the ritual, mythology and history of the Yucatan Peninsula, this calendrical system was no longer observed by the Postclassic peoples of the Maya highlands. Although widespread in Postclassic and colonial Yucatan, the concept of trees, colours and other features oriented to the four directions was little developed among the highland Maya. In addition, many of the sixteenth century gods recorded for the Quiché and other highland Mayan peoples cannot easily be identified in the writing and art of Postclassic and early colonial Yucatan.

In addition to having distinct customs and language, the Postclassic Maya were also politically diverse. At the time of the Spanish conquest there was no single great empire, as in the case of the Aztec, but many competing Maya states. Although the neighbouring Quiché and Cakchiquel spoke very similar languages, they were fierce enemies, and during the 1524 conquest of the Guatemalan highlands by Pedro de Alvarado, the Cakchiquel readily served as Spanish allies against the Quiché. Even the culturally homogeneous region of Yucatan was broken into a complex patchwork of competing city states and provinces at the time of Spanish contact and widespread unified resistance against foreign domination did not occur until well after the various groups had been subsumed under Spanish colonial rule.

Despite this regional diversity, many religious traits were shared between the various Postclassic Maya peoples. Some common elements seem relatively recent introductions from Postclassic central Mexico, which had close political and economic ties to the Maya region. An example is the central Mexican god

Quetzalcoatl, the plumed serpent, who was known by the Yucatec equivalent of Kukulcan and as Gucumatz by the highland Maya Quiché and Cakchiquel. Although of considerable importance in Postclassic Maya myth and legend, this god is virtually absent from Maya writing and art of the earlier Classic period. Another probable Postclassic introduction is the legendary western place of origin known as Zuyua by the Yucatec Maya and Tulan Zuiva by the Cakchiquel and Quiché. Clearly the highland Maya term links this place to Tollan of the Toltecs, now known to be the Early Postclassic site of Tula in Hidalgo.

Although certain specific traits found among both lowland and highland Maya peoples are comparatively recent Postclassic introductions from highland Mexico, the majority of shared religious elements derive from a deeper level of Maya culture and appear in the earlier Classic period writing and art of the Maya lowlands. Human sacrifice – often said to have originated in Postclassic central Mexico – is now known to have been widely practised by the Classic Maya. Another common Postclassic Maya form of sacrifice, penitential blood-letting from the tongue, penis and other parts of the body, is now recognised as one of the more common ritual themes in Classic Maya texts and monumental art. In addition to ceremonies, many of the gods and myths of the Postclassic Maya derive from earlier Classic traditions. The vast majority of major Maya deities known from the Postclassic codices of Yucatan, some fifteen in all, were already worshipped among the Classic Maya.

Perhaps the greatest deity of the ancient Maya was **Itzamna**, an old, wizened creator god similar to Tonacatecuhtli of central Mexico. Representations of Itzamna are widespread in both Classic and Postclassic Maya art. His consort seems to have been **Ix Chel**, an aged goddess identified with the roles of midwife and curer. Like Tlaloc, his central Mexican counterpart, the Maya god of rain and lightning, **Chac**, is one of the longest continuously worshipped gods in Mesoamerica. First known in Protoclassic Maya art dating to roughly the first century BC, Chac is still invoked in the mythology and prayers of modern Maya peoples. The ancient Chac wields serpents and axes, symbols of his lightning power.

Another major deity of the Classic and Postclassic Maya was the maize god. Surprisingly, his Postclassic name remains unknown, but there are indications that one important Classic form was named Hun Nal. In both form and

The old creator god, Itzamna, facing a tree with a caiman trunk. Detail of Late Classic Maya vase.

*Chac fishing with a net.
Izapa Stela 1,
Protoclassic Maya.*

symbolic domain, the ancient Maya death god was very similar to the central Mexican Mictlantecuhtli. One of the modern and Postclassic Maya terms for this skeletal deity is **Cizin**, meaning 'flatulent one', although he was also known as **Yum Cimih,** or Lord of Death. The name of the ancient sun god was **Kinich Ahau,** Sun-Faced Lord, a powerful being closely identified with the jaguar. It seems that this god transformed into a jaguar during his nightly journey through the underworld.

The early colonial *Popol Vuh* is perhaps the most striking example of Maya religious continuity from the Classic period to the sixteenth century. Recent research indicates that much of the creation mythology of the Quichean *Popol Vuh*, particularly the portion concerning the hero twins and their father, was known to the Classic Maya. Moreover, parts of this section can be traced back still earlier, to the Protoclassic site of Izapa. As it now stands, the Classic and Protoclassic scenes pertaining to the *Popol Vuh* constitute the oldest well-documented mythology of the New World.

The *Popol Vuh*: primordial origins

The first portion of the *Popol Vuh* movingly describes the creation of the world and its inhabitants out of the primordial sea and sky. Like the Aztec myth of the five suns, there are multiple creations and destructions, each associated with a particular race of people. Here, however, the series of human creations are fashioned and destroyed for a specific reason. According to the *Popol Vuh*, people are made to provide nourishment for the gods in the form of prayer and sacrifice. The concept of nourishment is taken quite literally in the *Popol Vuh*, and at one point the act of creation is described much like the preparation of a four-sided maize field with a measuring cord:

> The fourfold siding, the fourfold cornering,
> measuring, fourfold staking,
> halving the cord, stretching the cord
> in the sky, on the earth,
> the four sides, the four corners.

It is the people of maize, the product of this cosmic corn field, who finally provide sustenance for the gods.

Although little of the first section of the *Popol Vuh* is represented in the writing and art of the Classic Maya, this may be partly because it tends to deal with general cosmic abstractions rather than easily identified mythical episodes. The colonial Yucatec also conceived of the earth as a four-sided maize field. Many elements described in this beginning section of the *Popol Vuh*, such as multiple creations and the dualistic opposition of sky and earth, are probably among the most basic and ancient features of Mesoamerican religion.

The creation epic of the *Popol Vuh* begins with the vast, still expanse of the sea and sky before the creation of the earth:

There is not yet one person, one animal, bird, fish, crab, tree, rock, hollow, canyon, meadow, forest. Only the sky alone is there; the face of the earth is not clear. Only the sea alone is pooled under all the sky; there is nothing whatever gathered together. It is at rest; not a single thing stirs. It is held back, kept at rest under the sky.

Coiled within the water, surrounded by shimmering green and blue feathers, lies the plumed serpent Gucumatz. In the sky above is Heart of Heaven who, by his other name of Huracan, appears as three forms of lightning. Out of the still silence, Heart of Heaven and Gucumatz begin to speak to one another, discussing the creation, the first dawn and the making of people and their food. By their speech alone, the mountains and earth magically rise from the

The lightning deity God K, or Kauil, a possible aspect of Huracan. Detail of Late Classic Maya vase.

waters, and forests of cypress and pine instantly blanket the landscape.

To inhabit the newly made earth, the creators fashion birds, deer, jaguars, serpents – all the creatures of the forest mountains. After providing them with shelter, the creators ask the animals to praise and name them in prayer. But the animals are unable to speak:

They just squawked, they just chattered, they just howled. It wasn't apparent what language they spoke, each one gave a different cry.

Because the animals cannot speak properly and worship the gods, the creators decide that they will not be given dominion over the earth, but instead must remain in the wilds to be food for the people who *will* worship and sustain the gods.

For a second time, the creators try to fashion people, and they model one out of clay. But although it talks, its words make no sense and its body is weak and poorly made and soon begins to crumble and dissolve. Realising that it cannot survive or multiply, they break up the image, and begin yet again to create another form of people.

After their first two unsuccessful attempts, Heart of Heaven and Gucumatz consult the old diviner couple Xpiyacoc and Xmucane. Using maize grain and red seeds, the soothsayers cast lots while counting the days of the sacred calendar. They divine that humans should be made of wood and, upon hearing this, the creators say 'so be it', and instantly the world is populated by a race of wooden people. While the men are made of wood, the women are formed of rushes. Although they look, speak and multiply like people, they are dry, bloodless beings with expressionless faces. The wooden people lack souls and understanding, and do not respect or worship their creators. Concluding that they must be humiliated and destroyed, the gods create a great flood. A rain of resin falls from the sky, and fierce demons gouge and tear apart the wooden people. Even their utensils and animals rise up against them:

Into their houses came the animals, small and great.
Their faces were crushed by things of wood and stone.
Everything spoke: their water jars, their tortilla griddles, their plates, their cooking pots, their dogs, their grinding stones, each and every thing crushed their faces.

The wooden people try to flee but there is no refuge – everywhere they are pushed away and killed. The descendants of the race of wooden beings are the forest monkeys, left as a sign (and perhaps a warning) of this ancient, thoughtless creation.

Following the flood and the destruction of the wooden race, the earth is again devoid of humans. Still the gods lack beings to sustain them with prayer and offerings. Proper humans cannot be produced until the hero twins rid the world of demons and obtain the material from which human flesh is made.

The hero twins and the vanquishing of Xibalba

The second major portion of the *Popol Vuh* concerns the activities of two related sets of twins. The older twins, born of the soothsayers Xpiyacoc and Xmucane, are called by the calendrical dates of **Hun Hunahpu** (One Hunahpu) and **Vucub Hunahpu** (Seven Hunahpu). Hun Hunahpu has a pair of sons named **Hun Batz** and **Hun Chouen**, trained as great artists and performers by their father and uncle. **Xquic**, who is impregnated by Hun Hunahpu, gives birth to another pair of twins, **Xbalanque** and **Hunahpu**, the great hero twins who slay the monster bird **Vucub Caquix**. But their most spectacular victory is the defeat of the death gods and demons of Xibalba, the fearsome underworld.

Hun Hunahpu and Vucub Hunahpu are great gamesters who love to throw dice and play ball in their masonry ballcourt with Hun Hunapuh's sons, Hun Batz and Hun Chouen. Although it is on the earth, this ballcourt is also the path to the gloomy netherworld realm of Xibalba. The principal lords of Xibalba, Hun Came and Vucub Came (One Death and Seven Death), become enraged at the thundering noise from the ballgame above and call together all the gods and demons of death and disease to decide how to defeat and kill the twins. They send four owl messengers up to the surface to invite Hun Hunahpu and Vucub Hunahpu to play ball with them in Xibalba. Although their mother Xmucane tries to persuade them not to go, the two agree to follow the owls into the deadly underworld.

The path to Xibalba is long and treacherous, and the twins must pass obstacles such as fierce rapids, thorny spikes, and a river of blood. All these are successfully overcome until they reach a crossroads with four paths of different colours. They wrongly choose the black path, which marks the beginning of their undoing. When they arrive at Xibalba they greet the underworld lords, but in fact these are only wooden dummies dressed like the gods of death. The denizens of Xibalba roar with laughter, now certain of their victory. They invite Hun Hunahpu and Vucub Hunahpu to sit on a bench, which is no ordinary seat, but rather a searing hot slab of stone:

So now they were burned on the bench; they really jumped around on the bench now, but they got no relief. They really got up fast, having burned their butts. At this the Xibalbans laughed again, they began to shriek with laughter.

As a final test, the lords of Xibalba give the twins cigars and torches that must remain lit as well as intact all night while in the House of Gloom. At dawn, the gods of death find that the twins have failed this impossible task: the cigars and torches have burned away.

Tricked and overpowered by the lords of Xibalba, the twins are sacrificed and buried within the underworld ballcourt. As a token of their victory, the netherworld gods place the head of Hun Hunapuh in a barren tree. Instantly, this tree becomes laden with calabash gourds, with the head becoming one of the many round fruits. The underworld maiden Xquic hears of this miraculous gourd tree, and goes to see it for herself. The young woman asks herself aloud whether she should pick one of the fruits. The head of Hun Hunahpu hears

Xquic and tells her that the fruits are nothing but a crop of skulls. None the less, the maiden asks for the fruit. Spitting into her hand, the skull impregnates Xquic and tells her of his essence:

It is just a sign that I have given you, my saliva, my spittle. This, my head, has nothing on it – just bone, nothing of meat. It's just the same with the head of a great lord: it's just the flesh that makes his face look good. And when he dies, people get frightened by his bones. After that, his son is like his saliva, his spittle, in his being, whether it be the son of a lord or the son of a craftsman and orator. The father does not disappear, but goes on being fulfilled.

Eventually the father of Xquic notices her pregnant condition and demands to know who the father is. Although Xquic steadfastly denies having known a man, it is of no avail, and her father resolves to kill her. The messenger owls then take the maiden away to be sacrificed, but she convinces them to spare her. In place of her bloody heart, they return with a thick mass of resin, the blood of trees. Burning the resin incense, the death lords are entranced by its smell, and take no notice of the owls leading Xquic to the surface of the earth. In this way, the lords of Xibalba are tricked and defeated by the maiden.

Arriving at the home of Xmucane, the mother of the slain twins, Xquic declares herself to be her daughter-in-law, the wife of Hun Hunahpu. But

Death god ballplayer. Jaina style ceramic figurine, Late Classic Maya.

Xmucane, convinced that her sons are dead, wants nothing to do with the pregnant maiden. None the less, as a test, she sends Xquic to gather a netful of maize from the field of Hun Batz and Hun Chouen. Although the field has only a single maize plant, she returns with a great load of corn, and in so doing, proves that she is the wife of Hun Hunahpu.

Xquic gives birth to the hero twins Hunahpu and Xbalanque. Although they are the children of Hun Hunahpu, the twins are not well received by Xmucane, their grandmother, or by Hun Batz and Hun Chouen, who are jealous of their younger half-brothers. While the older brothers dance and make fine music and art, Hunahpu and Xbalanque roam the forest, shooting animals with their blow-guns. The spoiled older brothers snatch away all their game and leave them with only scraps of bone and gristle. One day the twins return with nothing, telling their brothers that the shot birds are caught high in a tree. Hun Batz and Hun Chouen agree to climb the tree but as they go up, the trunk miraculously swells and grows to a great height. The panicked elder brothers call out to Xbalanque and Hunahpu for help, who tell them: 'Untie your loincloths, wrap them around your hips, with the long end hanging like a tail behind you, and then you'll be able to move better.' Upon doing this, Hun Batz and Hun Chouen are turned into forest monkeys, tricked by their younger brothers Xbalanque and Hunahpu. But rather than being forgotten, these two monkeys become the patrons of artists, dancers and musicians.

After the great flood, a host of monstrous beings dwell on the surface of the world. The greatest is Vucub Caquix, Seven Macaw, a vainglorious bird who proclaims himself the sun and moon, lord over all. Angered by this false boasting, Hunahpu and Xbalanque decide to slay the monster bird. Hiding under his favourite fruit tree, the twins wait with their blow-guns, and when Vucub Caquix alights, Hunahpu shoots him in the face. Wounded and enraged, the bird tears off Hunahpu's arm and escapes with this trophy. Enlisting an old couple to pose as healers, the twins tell them to visit Vucub Caquix and offer to cure his aching eyes and teeth. The aged pair tell the monster bird that they must

The mosquito, an ally of the hero twins.
Detail from Late Classic Maya vase.

Camazotz, the killer bat. Detail from Chama style Late Classic Maya vase, Guatemala.

replace his teeth and eyes, but in place of his teeth they insert grains of corn. Once his eyes and teeth are gone, Vucub Caquix loses his glory and power, and quickly dies. Placing the severed arm of Hunahpu against the stump, the old couple heal the wound so that his arm is perfectly restored.

Like their father and uncle, the hero twins learn to play ball at the ballcourt. The lords of Xibalba are again infuriated by the incessant pounding above their heads and send their owls to summon the twins to the underworld. In their descent to Xibalba, Hunahpu and Xbalanque successfully pass rivers of pus and blood and other deadly obstacles until they come to the crossroads. Here Hunahpu plucks out a hair from his shin and creates a mosquito to spy ahead and bite the underworld lords. The insect first attacks the enthroned wooden images, but then finds the actual lords, and as they are bitten they cry out each other's names. In this way, the twins learn the names of all the underworld lords.

When Xbalanque and Hunahpu arrive at the palace of the underworld lords, they ignore the wooden statues and the burning hot seat and correctly greet all of the death gods by name. The astonished lords of Xibalba then send them with the cigars and torches to the House of Gloom. The twins cleverly place red macaw feathers on the torches and fireflies on the cigars to make them seem as if they are burning. At dawn the unburned fire brands and cigars are as new. The twins then play ball with the death gods, eventually allowing themselves to be beaten. That night they face another series of tests, but by their cunning they pass safely through the House of Knives, the House of Cold, the House of Jaguars and the House of Fire. Finally, they are sent to the House of Bats, a room filled with fierce knife-nosed bats. To protect themselves the twins hide inside their hollow blow-guns, but Hunahpu peeks out to see if dawn is approaching, and at that moment the killer bat Camazotz snatches off his head.

The head of Hunahpu is taken to the ballcourt and all of the death gods and demons rejoice, since their victory over the twins now seems all but certain.

However, in the late pre-dawn hours, Xbalanque calls on all the animals to bring their various foods. Some creatures present rotten things, others offer leaves and grasses. Finally, the coati (similar to a raccoon) arrives with a large squash, and Xbalanque places it against the severed neck of Hunahpu like a new head. Magically, the squash takes the form of Hunahpu's features, and he can see and speak. At dawn, the twins appear together at the underworld ballcourt as if nothing had happened.

The death gods begin the game by throwing out the real head of Hunahpu to serve as the new ball. Xbalanque strikes the head so hard that it bounces out of the court and into the woods. A rabbit, previously told to wait in the trees, immediately bounds away, confusing the death gods who mistake it for the ball. While their attention is distracted, Xbalanque retrieves Hunahpu's real head and places it back on his body. When the death gods return, the twins throw the squash into the court:

The squash was punted by Xbalanque, the squash was wearing out; it fell on the court, bringing to light its light-coloured seeds, as plain as day right in front of them.

Thus the confused and astonished death gods are truly defeated in their underworld court of sacrifice.

Although Xbalanque and Hunahpu are victorious, they know that the death gods will not rest until they are killed. The lords of Xibalba fashion a great fiery pit and invite the twins to jump over it. However, knowing that the death gods only want their deaths, the twins bravely jump into the pit and die. The gods of Xibalba then grind their charred bones and cast them into the river. The bones do not drift away but instead settle to the bottom, and in five days the twins reappear as fish-men. The following day they return to Xibalba disguised in rags as poor itinerant performers. Hearing of their wonderful dances, the lords of Xibalba command them to perform at their palace. After many dances, the twins are told to sacrifice a dog and then bring it back to life. This they do, and then they sacrifice a man and also bring him back to life. Xbalanque then decapitates Hunahpu and tears out his heart, only to restore him once again. The principal death gods, Hun Came and Vucub Came, are overjoyed and ecstatic at this miraculous dance and, in the throes of their enthusiasm, they ask to be killed. The twins kill one of them but they leave him dead and lifeless.

As soon as they had killed the one lord without bringing him back to life, the other lord had been meek and tearful before the dancers. He didn't consent, he didn't accept it:
'Take pity on me!' he said when he realised. All their vassals took the road to the great canyon, in one single mass they filled up the deep abyss.

Thus, through trickery and cunning, the twins completely vanquish the evil kingdom of Xibalba. Appearing before its defeated inhabitants, they reveal their true identities and threaten to slay everyone. The Xibalbans beg for mercy and tell them where their father and uncle are buried. The twins then agree to spare the people of Xibalba, but tell them that they will never again be powerful:

The Maya maize god. Stone sculpture (Museum of Mankind, London) from Temple 22, Copan, Honduras, Late Classic period.

All of you listen, you Xibalbans: because of this, your day and your descendants will not be great. Moreover, the gifts you receive will no longer be great, but reduced to scabrous nodules of sap. There will be no clearly blotted blood for you, just griddles, just gourds, just little things broken to pieces.

The twins then recover and speak to the remains of their father and uncle, reassuring them that they will continue to be respected and worshipped. Xbalanque and Hunahpu then rise into the heavens, where they become the sun and moon.

The origin of maize and people

Although the monstrous gods and demons of the earth and underworld had been destroyed, there were still no people to nourish the gods. In the pre-dawn darkness, Gucumatz and Heart of Heaven call on fox, coyote, parrot and crow to bring yellow and white maize from Paxil and Cayala, a mountain filled with seeds and fruits. Old Xmucane grinds the maize and, from the meal, the first four men are fashioned. Unlike the previous wooden race, these people of corn possess great knowledge and understanding and correctly give thanks to their creators. However, Gucumatz and Heart of Heaven are troubled; these corn men can see everywhere – through earth and sky to the limits of the universe. The creators decide that these people are too much like themselves, and that their powers must be diminished. As though they were breathing mist on a mirror, the gods blur the vision of the first people so that they can see clearly only what is near. In place of omniscience, the creators give the first men happiness by providing them with four beautiful wives to be their companions. With these four women, the first lineages of the Quiché are begun.

In darkness, the first tribes of the world journey to Tulan Zuiva, the place of Seven Caves and Seven Canyons. There they receive their various gods, including Tohil, a patron god of the Quiché and the source of fire. When the different peoples finally depart from Tulan with their gods, they no longer speak one language but many. In the dark pre-dawn hours, each group of people sets off in a different direction, with the Quiché going towards the west. While fasting and seeking the dawn, the Quiché look back to the east, the region of Tulan Zuiva. Finally the Quiché arrive at Mount Hacauitz, where they witness the dawn. At the appearance of the morning star, they joyfully offer incense to the east, and soon afterwards the sun appears:

The sun was like a person when he revealed himself. His face was hot, so he dried out the face of the earth. Before the sun came up it was soggy, and the face of the earth was muddy before the sun came up. And when the sun had risen just a short distance he was like a person, and his heat was unbearable.

At this moment the Quiché gods are turned to stone, along with the images of powerful animals such as the puma, jaguar and rattlesnake. Ever since the first dawn, therefore, this is how these images have been seen.

The *Popol Vuh* creation epic in Classic Maya religion

A great many of the characters and events mentioned in the portion of the *Popol Vuh* describing the hero twins are fully present in Classic Maya mythology, over seven hundred years before the sixteenth-century manuscript was written. Finely painted or carved ceramic vessels constitute the most valuable Classic source pertaining to the *Popol Vuh*. Most of the known Classic vessels derive from the lowland jungle Peten of Guatemala, centre of the Classic Maya area. Whereas Classic Maya stone monuments tend to focus upon historical individuals in scenes of personal aggrandisement, the vessel scenes are filled with allusions to mythical events. Although many of the mythical episodes appearing on Classic Maya pottery can be related to the *Popol Vuh*, events are also depicted which are not mentioned in the colonial Quiché text. These Classic episodes sometimes provide insights into the basic underlying meanings of the *Popol Vuh*.

    The Classic period counterpart of Hun Hunahpu, the father of the hero twins, is a form of the maize god. This deity is depicted with a flattened and elongated forehead, often accentuated by shaved zones delineating patches of hair on his brow and the top of his head. The elongated and shaved head imitates a ripened ear of corn, with the capping tuft of hair representing the silk at the tip of the cob. The removal of the ear from the stalk at harvest represents his decapitation, the same fate also meted out to Hun Hunahpu. On one Late Classic vessel the head of the maize god appears in a cacao tree; among the cacao pods above, one can discern a human head partially transformed into a cacao

The head of the maize god placed in a cacao tree. A second human head, partly transformed into a cacao pod, can be seen at upper right. Detail from Late Classic Maya vase (Museo Popol Vuh, Guatemala City).

fruit. This scene clearly portrays a version of the *Popol Vuh* incident in which the severed head of Hun Hunahpu is placed in a tree, although in this case the head has become a cacao pod rather than a calabash gourd.

The episodes illustrated for the Classic form of Hun Hunahpu are much more detailed and complex than what is contained in the early colonial *Popol Vuh*. In many cases, he is shown with bodies of standing water; this is probably a reference to Xibalba, since the ancient Maya regarded the underworld as a watery place. In one important episode, he stands in the water while being dressed in his finery by a group of nubile young women. Sometimes this event seems to have erotic overtones, although it is unknown whether these beautiful women are his wives. The women appear to be dressing him for a journey, and in a related episode he is being paddled in a canoe. Although this may be a journey to his death, it probably also refers to his eventual resurrection.

The Classic form of Hun Hunahpu is frequently portrayed as a dancer and artist. However, as in the *Popol Vuh*, it is not Hun Hunahpu but his sons, Hun Batz and Hun Chouen, who serve as the Classic patron gods of scribes. In Classic iconography, Hun Batz and Hun Chouen typically appear as monkeys (transformed by their half-brothers, Hunahpu and Xbalanque) wielding pens and cut-shell inkpots as they paint in screenfold books.

The hero twins Hunahpu and Xbalanque appear commonly in Classic Maya art and writing. Both usually wear the red and white cloth headband associated with Classic Maya rulership, and in fact the face of Hunahpu serves as a glyph for the day-name Ahau, a word meaning king in Mayan languages. Hunahpu is typically marked by large black spots on his cheeks and body. Xbalanque, on the other hand, displays jaguar skin patches around his mouth and on his torso and limbs. As well as appearing with their father and the monkey scribes, the twins are often shown with their blow-guns shooting down the Classic form of the monster bird Vucub Caquix. However, this bird is not a macaw but rather a mythical creature with serpent-faced wings and a long pendulous beak possibly based on the King Vulture.

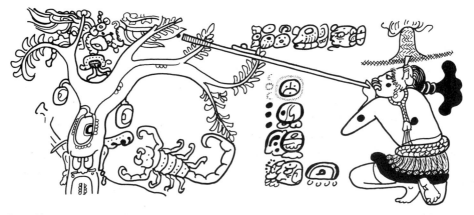

Late Classic Maya vessel scene, illustrating Hunahpu shooting Vucub Caquix out of his fruit tree.

The defeat of Vucub Caquix by the hero twins. Izapa Stela 2, Protoclassic period.

The monster bird slain by the hero twins is very common in Protoclassic Maya art, that is, around the beginning of Maya civilisation. The site of Izapa, situated in the southern coastal region of Chiapas, near the Guatemalan border, reveals that even at this early date the monster bird was clearly related to the *Popol Vuh* character. Dating to approximately the beginning of the Christian era, two Izapan monuments depict an especially early version of the Vucub Caquix episode. On Izapa Stela 2, the great bird descends to his fruit-laden tree; running towards the tree is a pair of human figures, probably the earliest known New World version of the hero twins. The monster bird appears again at the base of the fruit tree, in this case with a fleshless lower jaw and with his wing awkwardly bent under his body. The entire scene graphically represents the defeat of Vucub Caquix as he is struck down from his fruit tree by the hero

A possible representation of Hunahpu with his arm severed. Detail from Izapa Stela 25, Protoclassic period.

twins. The other Izapa monument, Stela 25, depicts the monster bird hovering above a male with only one arm; the other limb is clearly torn off, and blood is pouring from the severed stump. This scene probably concerns the battle in which Vucub Caquix tears off and escapes with the arm of Hunahpu.

As in the *Popol Vuh*, the hero twins are related to the ballgame in Classic Maya art. At the site of Copan, a stone marker from an actual ballcourt represents Hunahpu playing against a death god. On another Late Classic ballcourt marker, discovered near Chinkultic in highland Chiapas, a ballplayer dressed in death symbols strikes the ball with his hips. Lightly incised on the ball is the head of Hunahpu, recalling the *Popol Vuh* episode in which the death gods play with Hunahpu's head after snatching it from the House of Bats. These ballcourt markers reveal that the Classic Maya re-enacted in actual ballcourts the mythical game between the hero twins and the lords of Xibalba.

In one of the most common and important themes of the hero twins on Classic Maya pottery, they appear assisting their father, the maize god. In certain vessel scenes, the twins stand in water with the nude young women and hold the regalia of the maize god, such as his jewellery and a sack bundle. Certain scenes reveal that this sack contains maize grain, the essence of their

Late Classic vessel depiction of the emergence of the maize god out of the earth. On either side of the split turtle shell, a pair of Chac figures wield lightning weapons, including a burning, serpent-footed lightning axe at right.

father. In a related episode, the twins appear with the maize god as he rises out of a turtle shell. Among the ancient Maya, the turtle served as a metaphor for the earth floating upon the sea, and it is quite likely that this scene represents the maize god being resurrected from the earth. In one vessel scene, a pair of Chacs are brandishing lightning weapons as they flank the carapace. This represents the Maya version of the origin of maize from Tonacatepetl (see p. 39). In the Maya myth – still present today in the Maya area – the Chacs split open the maize rock with lightning.

Although it is not mentioned in the early colonial *Popol Vuh*, the resurrection of the maize god by the hero twins and the Chacs adds an important insight into the underlying meaning of the journey of the hero twins in search of their father. In addition to vengeance, their mission is to resurrect him from the underworld and thus bring maize to the surface of the earth. But this episode probably concerns more than just the origin of corn. In the Quichean *Popol Vuh*, the search for maize immediately follows the vanquishing of Xibalba and the partial revival of Hun Hunahpu and Vucub Hunahpu. This maize is the source of the modern race of humans, the people of corn. Thus, for the Classic period, the elaborate underworld journey of the maize god and his sons ultimately concerns the origin of people – the creation of mankind from corn. In both content and meaning it is very similar to the underworld descent of Quetzalcoatl to retrieve the bones from which people will be made. In the Aztec myth these bones were ground into meal by the aged goddess Cihuacoatl, and in the *Popol Vuh* episode old Xmucane grinds the corn from which people are eventually made.

Maya mythology of Yucatan

Unlike the highland Maya Quiché, there is very little mythological material available for the sixteenth-century Maya of the Yucatan Peninsula. Fray Diego de Landa does provide detailed information on Yucatec Maya ritual and calendrics, but regrettably he makes little mention of particular myths. The one exception is a short reference to sky-bearers and the flood (see p. 69). The three pre-Hispanic Yucatec books known as the Dresden, Madrid and Paris codices contain only oblique references to mythological episodes. The poorly understood 'serpent-numbers' section of the Codex Dresden refers to events in remote antiquity, before the present Baktun cycle era which began in 3114 BC. Like similarly ancient Classic period dates, these pre-3114 BC references probably concern such mythological events as the origins of particular gods and the creation of the present world. It is noteworthy that the pre-Hispanic forms of Xbalanque and Hunahpu are represented in the Yucatec codices, frequently in association with the maize god. Thus, although the contact-period form of the *Popol Vuh* epic is only preserved for the Quiché Maya, a version was probably also present among the Postclassic Maya of Yucatan.

The most important sources of ancient Yucatec Maya mythology are the native community manuscripts known as the Books of Chilam Balam. Dating to

A portion of a serpent-numbers passage. Chac and a rabbit sit in the mouths of serpents marked with numbers denoting vast units of time. Codex Dresden, p. 61.

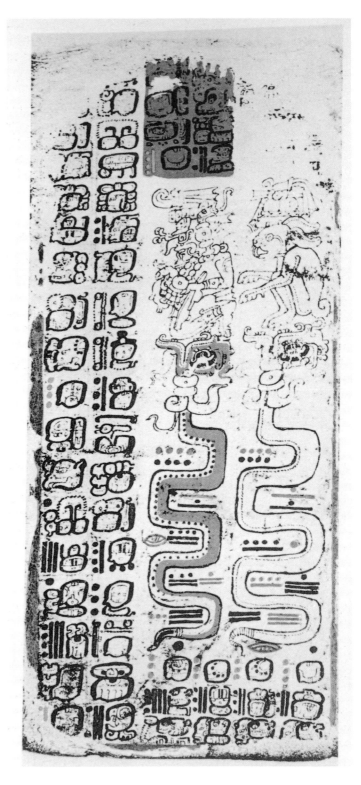

no earlier than the seventeenth century, the preserved myths are frequently placed in relation to calendrical cycles, particularly those based on the Maya Long Count. Although this may be distracting to the modern reader, it is a traditional lowland Maya convention for sacred narrative and is of respectable antiquity; mythological events in the Dresden serpent-number passages and Classic Maya inscriptions are presented in a similar fashion. Three Chilam Balam books, from the towns of Chumayel, Tizimin and Mani, contain virtually identical references to the flood and the restoration of the world. The passages contained in these Books of Chilam Balam share traits with Aztec creation mythology as well as with Landa's account and with the pre-Hispanic Codex Dresden.

Yucatec creation mythology and the flood

The sixteenth-century *Relación de las cosas de Yucatan* by Diego de Landa alludes to the flood in relation to four sky-bearers, known as Bacabs:

Among the multitude of gods which this nation worshipped they worshipped four, each of whom they called Bacab. They said that they were four brothers whom God placed, when he created the world, at the four points of it, holding up the sky so that it should not fall. They also said of these Bacabs that they escaped when the world was destroyed by the deluge.

These Bacab sky-bearers are probably forms of the ancient Maya god known as Pauahtun. Four-fold in nature, this aged being is frequently represented as a world-bearer in ancient Maya art and may personify sky-supporting mountains at the corners of the Maya world.

The accounts of the flood in the colonial Chilam Balam books can be understood as a creation event, as they lead directly to the origin of the present world. The principal protagonists are Ah Muzencab, possibly a god of bees, and Oxlahun-ti-ku and Bolon-ti-ku, whose names probably refer to the sky and underworld respectively, since the sky was believed to have thirteen (*oxlahun*) levels and the Underworld nine (*bolon*). In this episode, the flood is caused by Ah Muzencab and Bolon-ti-ku attacking Oxlahun-ti-ku and taking his regalia. Like the Landa account, both the Chumayel and Mani versions mention the Bacabs in relation to the flood:

There would be a sudden rush of water when the theft of the insignia of Oxlahun-ti-ku occurred. Then the sky would fall, it would fall down upon the earth, when the four gods, the four Bacabs, were set up, who brought about the destruction of the world.

As in the *Popol Vuh*, the Yucatec flood episode includes the destruction of an earlier, thoughtless race of people; however, the Yucatec texts do not specify the material from which this ancient race was made.

The Mani and Tizimin versions of the flood also mention the killing of a great earth caiman known as Itzam Cab Ain, Giant Fish Earth Caiman, which is identified with the earth as well as the flood. In both accounts, the caiman is slain by Bolon-ti-ku:

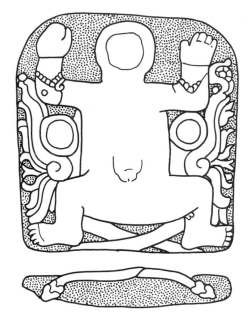

Yucatec Maya sculpture depicting Tlaltecuhtli with a pair of intertwined snakes. Mayapan, Late Postclassic period.

Then occurs the great flooding of the earth. Then arises the great Itzam Cab Ain. The ending of the world, the fold of the *katun*: that is a flood which will be the ending of the world of the *katun*. But they did not agree, the 9 Gods [Bolon-ti-ku]; and then will be cut the throat of Itzam Cab Ain, who bears the country on his back.

This episode is markedly similar to Aztec mythology, in which Tlaltecuhtli or a great caiman is slain to create the earth, and it is possible that this portion of the Maya flood account may have been a Postclassic central Mexican introduction. A sculpture from the Late Postclassic Yucatec site of Mayapan represents a form of the Aztec Tlaltecuhtli in its typical squatting pose. A pair of snakes accompany the figure, recalling the *Histoyre du Mechique* episode in which Tezcatlipoca and Quetzalcoatl dismember Tlaltecuhtli by transforming themselves into two serpents.

Immediately after the flood, five great trees are set up to the four directions and the centre to sustain the sky. In the three accounts, these world trees are associated with colours and birds as well as with directions. The following is the Chumayel description of this event:

After the destruction of the world was completed, they placed a tree to set up in its order the yellow cock oriole. Then the white tree of abundance was set up. A pillar of the sky was set up, a sign of the destruction of the world; that was the white tree of abundance in the north. Then the black tree of abundance was set up in the west for the black-breasted *pidzoy* to sit upon. Then the yellow tree of abundance was set up in the south, as a symbol of the destruction of the world, for the yellow-breasted *pidzoy* to sit upon, for the yellow cock oriole to sit upon, the timid *mut*. Then the green tree of abundance was set up in the centre of the world as a record of the destruction of the world.

In the Mani and Tizimin versions, the first of the trees stands at the east and is red. The Mani also mentions that this first eastern tree, the Chac Imix Che, supports the sky and is a sign of the dawn.

Codex Dresden, p. 74,
a probable representation
of the flood.

Creation mythology and calendrics in Yucatan

It has already been noted that much of the creation mythology found in the Books of Chilam Balam is couched in terms of calendrics. For example, the three cited versions of the flood and the creation of the world occur in Katun 11 Ahau, which is the first of thirteen roughly twenty-year Katuns which repeat in a cycle of approximately 260 years. Individually named by the 260-day date on which they end, the thirteen Katuns invariably end on the day-name Ahau and begin on the day-name Imix (corresponding to the Aztec day-name Cipactli, or caiman). Although they are given varying colour designations, the trees set up after the flood are all termed Imix Che, or Imix trees, probably alluding to the first day in a new Katun cycle.

Not only are creation events described in terms of calendrical cycles, but calendrical rituals frequently express creation episodes. Landa's account of the flood and the Bacab sky-bearers is actually a preface to a detailed discussion of Yucatec Maya new year celebrations marking the completion and renewal of the 365-day vague year. The pre-Hispanic Codex Dresden contains a very similar situation: the scene on Dresden page seventy-four has been widely interpreted as representing world destruction and the flood. A partly reptilian skyband spouting three great channels of water dominates the upper portion of the scene. Below, the aged goddess Chac Chel (Ix Chel) pours water from a jar, and a black god, probably Chac, brandishes weapons. As well as mentioning the names Bacab, Chac and Chac Chel, the accompanying text also refers to black sky and black earth, probably a reference to world destruction.

The new year erection of the world tree of the west. Codex Dresden, p. 27.

In the original pagination of the Codex Dresden, page seventy-four immediately precedes the pages concerning the installation of the new year as described by Landa. One of the primary events in these four pre-Hispanic new year pages is the erection of four world directional trees, the first being the red tree of the east. Like Landa's account of the flood, page seventy-four introduces the new year ceremony in terms of world destruction and renewal, with the setting up of the trees signifying world renewal. The new year celebrations were annual ritual re-enactments of the destruction and re-creation of the world. The graphic accounts of the flood and the erection of world trees in the three Books of Chilam Balam reveal that the ritual installation of the Katun and other Long Count periods were thought of in very similar terms.

Rather than being unique to the Maya area, the documented mythology of the ancient Quiché and Yucatec shares many traits with Aztec myths. Like the Aztec, the Postclassic Maya of Yucatan and highland Guatemala believed in previous worlds, and that a flood immediately preceded the creation of the present era. The underworld descent of Xbalanque and Hunahpu in search of their father and their defeat of the gods of death recall the netherworld journey of Quetzalcoatl to retrieve the bones of the previous creation. Classic Maya art suggests that the underlying meaning of both the Quiché and Aztec myths is much the same. It seems that, in both cases, the descent to the underworld is a quest for the substance from which mankind is made. Classic Maya depictions of the hero twins' resurrection of their father reveal the considerable antiquity of the Maya version, showing that it was not a relatively recent introduction from central Mexico.

Certain aspects of Maya mythology do derive from Postclassic central Mexico. Thus the *Popol Vuh* mentions the plumed serpent Gucumatz and the city of Tollan. The Yucatec Itzam Cab Ain episode is clearly related to the Aztec myth describing the dismemberment of the earth monster. The previously mentioned Mayapan sculpture of the squatting earth monster suggests that the

A possible Classic representation of the flood caiman, reminiscent of the reptilian skyband which appears on p. 74 of the Codex Dresden. Detail from Late Classic Maya vase.

Maya of Yucatan were aware of Aztec mythology and even iconographic conventions. However, the Classic Maya may well have also conceived of a great earth caiman associated with the flood. One surviving Late Classic Maya vessel depicts a caiman with death and water markings suspended from the sky, recalling the reptilian skyband on page seventy-four of the Codex Dresden. The date associated with this scene is 4 Ahau 8 Cumku, which marks the beginning of the present great Baktun cycle beginning in 3114 BC. Could this Long Count event constitute a Classic version of the flood and the subsequent re-creation of the world? If so, the Classic period setting up of stone stelae at important Long Count intervals could be ritual re-enactments of the erection of world trees at the creation of the present era.

Mesoamerican mythology

In the recorded creation accounts of ancient Mesoamerica, the myths rarely stray far from the natural world. There is frequent mention of gods of wind, lightning, water, celestial bodies and other natural phenomena. Processes related to the agricultural cycle play an especially important role and, according to the *Popol Vuh*, the very flesh of humans was fashioned from maize. It is readily apparent from these sources that humans have an inherent responsibility – literally, a blood debt – to the gods who make existence possible. The repeating series of world creations and destructions is a continual reminder of the consequences of neglecting this obligation.

Calendrics and astrology served as basic templates for organising and observing the processes of the natural world, and thus it is not surprising that they too play a prominent role in ancient Mesoamerican mythology. Myths of world creations and destructions are frequently couched in terms of calendrical events. This is especially true for Late Postclassic Yucatan, where imagery of world destruction and renewal is repeatedly used to express the calendrical completion of the 365-day year and the Katun cycle. But the Mesoamerican relationship between calendrical events and myth is not simply metaphoric: the calendrical cycles were used to predict potential periods when the world might be destroyed. These calendrical period endings were seen as powerful and frightening times of living myth, when the gods and other forces of creation and chaos would again do battle in the world of mortals.

Ancient Mesoamerican calendrics, astrology and mythology were thus integrated into a single compelling system of belief. During the Aztec new fire vigil, marking the completion of a fifty-two year calendar round cycle, the inhabitants of Tenochtitlan would look anxiously to particular star groups to see if the world would continue or be destroyed. The profound influence on Mesoamerican life of the movements of the sun, stars, planets and other celestial bodies was also reflected in the mythology. Such celestial beings as Tlahuizcalpantecuhtli, Mixcoatl and Tonatiuh appear widely in central Mexican myth. Recent research by Linda Schele and David Freidel suggests that the Classic Maya version of the journey of the hero twins and their father through dark Xibalba was played out every year in the procession of constellations across the ecliptic – that is, the same annual path observed in the Old World zodiac of constellations. In support, they note that in a number of Mayan languages the Milky Way galaxy is referred to as Xibal Be, the road of Xibalba. These ongoing investigations present the intriguing possibility that the apparent movements of the stars and planets may have served as a basic structural model for the development of Mesoamerican mythology.

Compared with the Old World mythologies of Mesopotamia, Egypt or Greece, far less is known of the ancient myths of Mesoamerica. It is clear that we now understand only a fraction of the mythology present at the time of the conquest, and much less of myths of the Classic period. As has been noted, the dismemberment of Tezcatlipoca by Xiuhtecuhtli on page one of the Fejérváry-Mayer is not recorded in the myths of ancient central Mexico, and this is also true of many episodes illustrated in the middle pages of the Codex Borgia. For the Classic Maya, many vessel scenes illustrate obvious mythical episodes that bear no direct relationship to the *Popol Vuh* or other mythologies of the Post-classic, colonial or contemporary Maya. An excellent example, appearing on a number of polychrome vessels, is the theft by a rabbit of an old god's broad hat and other regalia. Not even the Maya name for the aged deity is known, and currently he is simply referred to as God L.

However, it is unlikely that such myths of the Classic Maya are lost forever. Great advances have been made recently in the decipherment of Maya hieroglyphs, and it is at last possible to read the names and deeds of particular gods. For ancient Maya studies, the current situation is much like the nineteenth-century flood of insights and interpretations that followed the decipherment of Egyptian hieroglyphs and Mesopotamian cuneiform. The next few decades therefore promise to be an extremely exciting time for the study of ancient Maya religion.

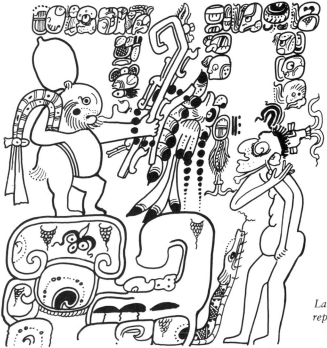

Late Classic Maya vessel scene, representing a rabbit seizing the clothes and regalia of the old God L.

Scene illustrating the resurrection of the maize god, the Classic form of Hun Hunahpu, out of the earth, symbolised by a turtle shell. His two sons, Hunahpu and Xbalanque, are shown assisting their father, and all three are accompanied by their identifying name glyphs. Interior of a Late Classic Maya ceramic bowl.

Unlike the Old World myths of Mesopotamia, Egypt and Greece, many of the mythic episodes and their protagonists mentioned in this book are still a part of contemporary Mesoamerican mythology. The adventures of Nanahuatzin continue to be invoked by Nahuat-speaking peoples living in the Sierra de Puebla. The myths of the Cora and Huichol of western Mexico share many similarities with known Aztec mythology. Just as the Classic Maya version of the *Popol Vuh* can shed light on the Quichean epic, contemporary myths often provide crucial insights into frequently laconic contact-period texts. Modern myths of the Kekchi, Mopan and other Maya peoples frequently contain episodes and motifs related to the *Popol Vuh*. This is also true for contemporary myths of the Mixe, Popoluca and Totonac of Oaxaca and Veracruz, which provide resonating parallels with the *Popol Vuh*, frequently concerning the origin of the maize god. Although modern Mesoamerican myths do often contain elements that are not pre-Hispanic in origin – such as Catholic saints and relatively recent historical events – these are not indications of a dying or decadent mythical tradition, but rather proof of a thriving oral legacy that continues to respond to a constantly changing world.

Suggestions for further reading

Mesoamerican religion is a vast and complex topic, and there are relatively few works encompassing the entire subject. *Religions of Mesoamerica* by D. Carrasco (San Francisco, 1990) provides a general overview of Mesoamerican religion, including two chapters devoted to Aztec and Maya ritual and belief. Incorporating introductory chapters on Mesoamerican religion, *Gods and Symbols of Ancient Mexico and the Maya* by M. Miller and K. Taube (London, 1993) presents the reader with an illustrated encyclopaedia of relevant religious terminology. The *Flayed God* by R. Markman and P. Markman (San Francisco, 1992) focuses specifically upon Mesoamerican mythology and contains translations of early colonial texts. Yet another text devoted to Mesoamerican mythology, *The Mythology of Mexico and Central America* by J. Bierhorst (New York, 1990), is a valuable synthesis of both ancient and contemporary Mesoamerican mythology.

For Aztec and central Mexican religion, the voluminous contributions of E. Seler remain indispensable. An English version of his massive compilation of studies, the *Gesammelte Abhandlungen zur Amerikanischen Sprach-und Altertumskunde*, is currently being published, with three volumes now available (Culver City, Calif., 1990–2). An excellent discussion of Aztec world view and philosophy is to be found in *Aztec Thought and Culture* by M. León-Portilla (Norman, Okla., 1963). *The Great Temple of the Aztecs* (London, 1988) by Matos Moctezuma provides a thorough discussion of the Huitzilopochtli myth and the recent excavations at the Templo Mayor.

Of the primary colonial sources pertaining to Aztec religion, the Florentine Codex is of central importance. An excellent English translation is provided by A. Anderson and C. Dibble (Santa Fe, New Mex. and Salt Lake City, Utah, 1950–82). A recent translation of the Nahuatl *Leyenda de los soles* is to be found in *History and Mythology of the Aztecs: The Codex Chimalpopoca* by J. Bierhorst (Tucson, Ariz., 1992). The *Historia de los mexicanos por sus pinturas* and the *Histoyre du Mechique* can be found in *Teogonía e historia de los Mexicanos* by A. M. Garibay (Mexico City, 1965).

The decipherment of Maya hieroglyphic writing is essential for the study of ancient Maya religion. Two recent discussions of the history of decipherment and the nature of Maya hieroglyphic writing are to be found in *Maya Glyphs* by S. Houston (London and Berkeley, 1989) and *Breaking the Maya Code* by M. Coe (London, 1992). For an introduction to some of the recent advances in the study of Classic Maya writing and religion, *The Blood of Kings* by L. Schele and M. Miller (Fort Worth, Tex., 1986 and London, 1992) is highly recommended. *The Major Gods of Ancient Yucatan* by K. Taube (Washington, DC, 1992) describes the identities and iconography of ancient Maya deities. An excellent corpus of Maya vase scenes with accompanying essays entitled *The Maya Vase Book* is currently being published by J. Kerr, with three volumes now available (New York, 1989, 1990, 1992).

A number of translations of the *Popol Vuh* are available, and two highly recommended versions are by A. Recinos (Norman, 1950) and D. Tedlock (New York, 1985). *Landa's Relación de las Cosas de Yucatan* by A. Tozzer (Cambridge, Mass., 1941) is not only a useful translation of the Landa document, but also provides a great deal of relevant information regarding Late Postclassic Yucatec religion. Of the colonial Yucatec Books of Chilam Balam, the books of Chumayel, Tizimin and Mani are best known. For the Chumayel, the edition by R. Roys (Norman, 1967) is highly recommended. M. Edmonson (Austin, Tex., 1982) has supplied a complete translation of the Tizimin. An English version of the Mani has been published by E. Craine and R. Reindorp in *The Codex Pérez and the Book of Chilam Balam of Maní* (Norman, 1979).

There are many important studies describing myths and legends of contemporary Mesoamerica, and many of the published accounts can be related to pre-Hispanic mythology. Two valuable publications relating to Nahua mythology of highland Mexico are *Nahuat Myth and Social Structure* by J. Taggart (Austin, 1983) and *Mitos y cuentos Nahuas de la Sierra Madre Occidental*, a compilation of texts collected by K. Preuss in 1907 (Mexico City, 1982). For myths of modern Maya peoples, the Tzotzil of Chiapas are particularly well represented, and *Chamulas in the World of the Sun* by G. Gossen (Cambridge, Mass., 1974) and *Of Cabbages and Kings* by R. Laughlin (Washington, DC, 1977) are two important works. A compilation of Yucatec Maya accounts can be found in *An Epoch of Miracles* by A. Burns (Austin, 1983).

Picture credits

Front cover: photo Justin Kerr; *p. 6*: Sergio Ransford; *p. 9*: Trustees of the British Museum, St.536; *p. 12*: Bodleian Library, Oxford, MS. Arch. Selden. A. 1, f. 2r; *pp. 14, 15*: Akademische Druck-und Verlagsanstalt, Graz; *p. 17 (right)*: BM St.399; *p. 19*: Akademische Druck-und Verlagsanstalt; *p. 21*: Sahagún, *Historia general de las cosas de Nueva España*, 1905–9; *p. 26*: León y Gama, *Descripción histórica y cronológica de las dos piedras que se hallaron en la Plaza Principal de México*, 1832; *p. 30*: BM 1974. AM8; *p. 32*: BM 1825. 12–10. 11; *pp. 35, 38*: Akademische Druck-und Verlagsanstalt; *p. 43 (top)*: Dr Emily Umberger; *p. 46*: photo Irmgard Groth-Kimball; *p. 48*: Sahagún, *Historia general de las cosas de Nueva España*, 1905–9; *p. 57*: Alice Wesche; *p. 61*: BM 321–1886; *p. 68*: American Philosophical Society, Philadelphia; *p. 71*: Akademische Druck-und Verlagsanstalt.

If not otherwise credited, photographs and line drawings are by Karl Taube.

Index